What Is This Prayer Stuff Anyway?

What Is This Prayer Stuff Anyway?

An Exploration of How Prayer Is More Than Words

LAURA MARIE PIOTROWICZ
RICK PRYCE

WIPF & STOCK · Eugene, Oregon

WHAT IS THIS PRAYER STUFF ANYWAY?
An Exploration of How Prayer Is More Than Words

Wipf & Stock
An Imprint of Wipf and Stock Publishers
199 W. 8th Ave., Suite 3
Eugene, OR 97401

www.wipfandstock.com

PAPERBACK ISBN: 979-8-3852-7228-0
HARDCOVER ISBN: 979-8-3852-7229-7
EBOOK ISBN: 979-8-3852-7230-3

VERSION NUMBER 02/13/26

To all those people of faith and prayer, who encouraged and inspired us along the way: family, friends, clergy, colleagues, and strangers, this book is most humbly and gratefully dedicated.

Contents

Introduction

WHY ARE WE DOING THIS?

We met as neighbors in small-town Nova Scotia, and as our friendship developed, we discovered a shared commitment and appreciation for prayer as a central feature of our spiritual journeys. In our many conversations, we shared with one another some of the joys and challenges in our prayer practice—and our desire to be more intentional about our prayers. This called for us to go deeper in our understanding and articulation of our relationship with prayer.

So, with some study, some contemplation, and much laughter, we decided to write this book as an exploration of prayer. We know that churchgoers (especially ministers!) are often presumed to be adept and committed to prayer, regularly called upon to say prayers at family gatherings, meals, at times of sickness or vulnerability, and of course, Sunday morning worship.

That being said, we are acutely aware that the act of prayer is not always understood or undertaken, by ourselves and others. We have too many anecdotes of hearing "I don't know how to pray" and "I don't have time to pray," even from church leaders. It is taken for granted that church membership indicates comfort and facility of any manner of divine conversation. In all honesty, we are aware of our own hesitancies and resistance in our own prayer lives. Our pastoral hearts found this book to be a way to gently engage ourselves to go deeper, and to invite others along the way.

SOME BACKGROUND

We started with the most basic question of all: Why do we pray?

There are, of course, any number of possible responses to this question, and we found it helpful to engage in the effort of trying to articulate some of our reasons.

But we discovered in a hurry that it is no easy task. Once we began trying to express *in words* what prayer is and why we try (or want) to pray, we realized that our vocabularies are woefully inadequate. As many prayerful authors have declared over the centuries, we might as well ask, "Why do we breathe?"

This is not a sarcastic response! This is an acknowledgment that the deeper we explore those things that define us as people, as human beings, as children of God, the harder it becomes to actually articulate an authentic, let alone accurate, answer.

And yet, we also believe we are called to wrestle with this question, not simply to verbalize *the* definition of prayer but to join the journey with others, who have been called to go deeper into the mystery and reality of prayer.

So, why *do* we pray?

Here are a few of the suggestions we came up with (in no particular order):

- to connect to the source of love and grace
- to express, as well as discover, who we are
- to make an effort at honest humility
- to care for the soul
- to verbalize the grief we are carrying
- to express care and concern for others
- to give voice to our gratitude

As we continued this exercise, we realized that part of prayer is also receiving from the One with whom we are praying:

- We can gain some perspective on the complexities of life.
- We can begin to recognize our giftedness.
- We can discover stillness and quiet in a world of noise and busyness.
- We can learn a deeper form of trust.
- We can be empowered to discover and use our voice.

- We can be formed into a more authentic community.
- We can go into the hard parts of life, surrounded by the promise that we are not alone.

Naturally, these suggestions only scratched the surface of possibilities. But they started the conversation and led us to recognize that the question of *why* is amplified by the other "W" questions of our school days: who, what, when, and where. While the "how" question will formulate the basis for most of the chapters later in this book, we were both aware of something stirring within us at that point.

The result of our conversations was a mutual discernment of a desire to collaborate in the development of a resource: for ourselves, for our communities, and beyond. We recognize that a book on prayer is not a new creation; each of us has a large collection of books, paper files, websites, and other prayer resources that guide and direct our spiritual journey. However, in our bookstore wish lists, the expense of multiple volumes can be prohibitive to a careful budget. (Also, some of these volumes are not available through our local libraries, and we suspect they would not appreciate our inclination to underline or highlight!)

We are called and privileged to lean into the intention to "read, mark, learn, and inwardly digest" the Scriptures and prayers, as they accompany and guide us in our faith expressions.[1] Many prayer books remain in regular use, so much so that they may appear dog-eared (or, in more than one case, puppy-chewed), fall open to particular often-visited pages, and at times, shed pages when we least expect it. The distinctive character of these volumes speaks of their place in our prayer lives.

Other books remain under-utilized (*read: collecting dust*) on our shelves, as we confess that despite our best intentions, we fail to dive deeply into such material. This can be for any number of reasons, from a lack of time or focus or insufficient energy to open a thick volume, to a (mis)perception of how much energy a new book and practice may demand of us. The attractive covers and engaging synopses can be easily overlooked on

1. In the Anglican *Book of Common Prayer*, Thomas Cranmer wrote this collect for the second Sunday of Advent: "Blessed Lord, who hast caused all holy Scriptures to be written for our learning: Grant that we may in such wise hear them, read, mark, learn, and inwardly digest them, that by patience and comfort of thy holy Word, we may embrace and ever hold fast the blessed hope of everlasting life, which thou hast given us in our Saviour Jesus Christ. Amen." Anglican Church of Canada, *Book of Common Prayer*, 97.

the shelf when balancing meal planning, dog walking, meetings, and every other factor that compromises the general busyness of life.

Further, as good as these prayer books are (and, wow, are some of them great!), there are times when they do not echo the prayers that our hearts crave, or when other people's words don't fully speak to our own prayerful desires or longings. This is not a criticism of these words, for many are rich, deep, and inviting, but is rather an acknowledgement that the Spirit may be doing something different in us at that moment.

As well, part of any genuine prayer journey is admitting that we experience "dry spells," where a particular style of prayer is not presently "working" as we would want it to work, or perhaps as it *used* to work. One way of responding may be to discover a new style or practice of prayer.

In response to all this holy prompting, we created this single volume, which introduces many prayer styles and practices, as a sampling of opportunities. Our intention is not to provide one-size-fits-all answers but a non-judgmental companion on the journey. It does not presume to know what you need to continue, revitalize, or even begin your prayer life, but recognizes the engagement in prayer you already have. It also realizes that it does not establish a connection with God but responds to the existing relationship we have with the One who invites us to pray.

We hope that this journey will highlight that we are, in fact, praying more often and more deeply than we realize, and that these practices may assist in articulating our intentionality of naming/claiming our daily actions as prayerful experiences.

Welcome, wherever you are on your ~~spiritual~~ spirited[2] journey!

WHAT DOES PRAYER LOOK LIKE? *AND* WHAT DOES THIS PRAYER RESOURCE LOOK LIKE?

Throughout the Scriptures, God's people are constantly seeking to learn to pray. Throughout the Gospels (especially Matt 6, Luke 11, and John 17), Jesus is teaching his friends and followers not only *how* to pray but to *deepen* their prayer practice.

This is a thread which runs throughout the history of God's faith-filled people, and one in which we find ourselves: not just wanting a teaching *about* prayer but finding a way of making the practice *of* prayer our own.

2. See upcoming, "A Note About Vocabulary."

The intentionality of prayerful practice is frequently described as a *regula* or rule of prayer. Theologian Martin Thornton describes it this way: "Prayer must be seen as a theological complex of life, a spiritual and recollective continuum made up of a totality of prayers, offices, meditations, liturgical actions and the rest. It is an overall pattern of life, a system, or to use the technical term, a *Regula*."[3]

Historically, this has taken the shape of fixed-hour or ordered prayers. Phyllis Tickle's book series *The Divine Hours* embraces this system of fixed-hour prayers as a means to integrate prayer into everyday life.[4] She bases the importance of this practice on biblical and other traditional models, such as,

- the first apostolic miracle (Acts 3:1), which occurred as Saints Peter and John were headed to the ninth-hour (3:00 p.m.) prayers;
- St. Peter's vision of the animal-laden sheet descending from heaven (called one of the great defining events of Christianity), which occurs during the sixth hour (noon) prayers;
- the use of psalms in regular prayer in the earliest Christian community in Acts 4:23–30;
- the *Didache* (an early instruction manual for prayer), which invites readers to pray the Lord's Prayer at least three times a day;
- modern prayer sources, such as the Anglican *Book of Alternative Services* and Lutheran *Evangelical Lutheran Worship*, which follow this pattern with the (more popular) morning and evening prayers offered alongside lesser-used liturgies, like prayers at midday and compline/night prayer.

At the same time, our modern world encourages us to ask questions and explore alternatives. We live in a society of highly literate, internet search-engine savvy, multicultural, intelligent people, who are free to explore a plethora of spiritual and religious offerings (which is easier than ever in our post-COVID world, where so much is now available online).

With that as our context, we found that exploring a variety of prayer practices can be helpful in working toward establishing our own *Regula* or pattern for prayer.

3. Thornton, *Function of Theology*, ch. 1.
4. Tickle, *Divine Hours*.

While Martin Thornton, writing in the context of 1950s western society, would compare spiritual nourishment to a banquet (at which the same meal is formally presented to all in attendance), this resource offers more of a spiritual buffet (at which participants make their own selections, based on what works for each). It is important to note that in both analogies, spiritual nourishment is available to those who are hungry. Regardless of the style of nourishment that is chosen by the participant (whether on a plate or in a prayer), it is noteworthy that participants are incorporating their own choices *and* that they are feasting within a community.

To facilitate this process, each of our chapters provides resources for the exploration of a variety of prayer practices. These include prayers that are classical and contemporary, silent and audible, word-based and action-based, contemplative and expressive, inward-focused and outward-focused, individual and corporate, ordinary and extraordinary.

These are designed to be practiced in any number of ways—alone, with families, or in small groups. This resource is intended to eliminate stigma or judgment, and you are encouraged to engage in some form of spiritual relationship with a trusted friend or director. It is also hoped that by providing such a resource, gatherings of people who pray together over time will increasingly become safe spaces to discuss matters of spiritual and prayerful importance. This resource is not intended to be a completed volume but rather a beginning point, which can be added to as its use leads to additional resources.

While the word *expert* means one who speaks out of experience, we don't consider ourselves experts in prayer. We know that prayer is not a completed action or process, and so, we speak and write as people who regularly experience the struggles and joys of prayer and strive to improve our practice as we go along.

As practitioners of prayer, we are familiar with the process of forming, amending, and readapting *Regulae* throughout our lives and ministries, including trying new things to see if they work for us. Some do, some don't; some are adapted into long practices while others are short-term or special-occasion practices. The importance for us is the willingness to try a new prayer experience.

To that end, each of the following chapters will provide some background of the particular style of prayer, then offer a few examples of how to incorporate this into your own prayer life. These are neither exclusive nor extensive. We are hoping this resource will provide for you a buffet of prayerful practices, that it may be filling for now, and also encourage you to explore other options as well!

A NOTE ABOUT VOCABULARY

We hear people both inside and outside of faith communities use the word "spiritual," but in discussion with various people, it becomes clear that we can mean vastly different things. Not to dismiss anyone's perspective, but to clarify ours, we think it is important to explain how we are using some of these terms.

The word "spiritual" originates in the biblical languages of ancient Hebrew and Greek, in which the words *ruach* and *pneuma*, meaning air or wind, were translated as *spiritus* for the Latin-speaking early church. Medieval Latin came to understand "the spirit" as anything that pertains to the divinely-provided life-force within the body, evidenced by the very act of breathing.[5]

As Old English developed, this understanding became related to the (archaic) word "godcundlic," which addresses things that pertain to the divine, are steeped in mystery, and are inspired by, or proceed from, God. This calls to mind one of the church's historic statements of faith, in which we confess that the Holy Spirit proceeds (literally "goes forward") from the Father.[6]

Language changes and evolves to address new people in new situations; we understand this. But we also want to be clear that our emphasis, as people who want to engage in the practice of prayer, is on the *godcundlic* sense of spirituality: God breathing the divine life into and through us.

Therefore, we propose to use the word *spirited*: the essence of our beings is not only lively but "life-ly," carrying the animation and enthusiasm that comes from the breath of God: giving life to all things, sustaining our bodies, and driving our prayers and praise.

5. Note that "spirit" is different from what later came to be called "the soul." The difference is subtle but, for our purposes, important.

6. In some traditions, "from the Father and the Son."

A NOTE ABOUT MULTI-FAITH AND INTERFAITH ISSUES

As will be seen, some of the prayer styles we suggest have been influenced or inspired by the practices of other traditions, cultures, and faiths.

We want to be very clear here. We are not attempting to co-opt other spiritual traditions and make them into something they are not. Nor are we pretending that all spiritual traditions are interchangeable. We *do* want to suggest that praying while using practices developed in other traditions can be an opportunity to engage in spiritual realities in new and life-giving ways.

Your authors are both practitioners within the Christian tradition. We have both experienced much life and faith affirmation from this tradition.

At the same time, we have both experienced much life and faith affirmation from the various interfaith encounters in which we have taken part. There are points of connection between almost all religious traditions and spiritual practices, just as there are points of divergence. Awareness of the former does not preclude the latter, nor does the presence of the latter negate the former. There are things to be gained from authentic encounters with "the other," which could not have happened if they had not taken place. And generally speaking, we find that we learn much more about our*selves* and *our* tradition in these encounters, which is always a good thing.

Much has been written about Christians who engage in spiritual practices that have origins in other places, times, and cultures. Some have embraced this engagement, welcoming the opportunity to explore a different way of embodying their faith. At the same time, there are those who have described participation in something that is not specifically of Christian background as "dangerous."[7]

While we admit that participation in (quite literally) anything of a "spiritual" nature can be challenging (especially if we are clinging too closely to our own *status quo*), we also have experienced, and very much affirm, that the love of God goes with us and frequently even leads us *into* those experiences. We can approach them as a chance to explore our faith in a different way, remembering the hundreds of times the biblical writers tell us not to be afraid, even when looking into something outside our previous experience (like new ways of praying!).

We invite you to join us in thanking God for the gift of inspiration, and we pray that you fearlessly dive in to new expressions of prayer.

7. See Varshney, "Cultural Appropriation," and Woods, "Yoga."

Chapter 0.5

Schrödinger's Prayer (or Not!)

The thought experiment of Erwin Schrödinger may be the only theory of quantum physics that many of us can cite: a theoretical cat in a box could be either alive or dead, or both, depending on the state of a release of poison in the box that may or may not occur. Thus, Schrödinger's cat is used colloquially when the outcome of something is not known, knowable, or possibly even understood.

Prayer can be like the hypothetical cat: alive or dead, or both, influenced by an external reality that may or may not have happened. Definitely, it is not always known, or knowable, or understood.

We often have conversations where folks share a concern of not knowing how to pray. This could mean unfamiliarity with written prayers or expected postures; it could be shyness about being called upon to pray publicly or a discomfort with preconceived notions of religion. (I was once at an awkward formal meal when a man said, "You're the one with religion—*you* pray!") Thus, Schrödinger enters in. (At least, his cat does, meandering confidently across our keyboards.)

Praying in one particular format or posture or tradition can be prayer, or it can not be prayer. Sometimes, it can be both. The act of prayer depends on the intention of the heart. Saying the words of a written prayer may be recitation or reading or research; or it may be prayer. Folding our hands together whilst kneeling in front of a cross may be prayer, or it may be something altogether different.

The way that we approach prayer is unique to each of us, and it can change over time (and time can be seconds or decades). It can differ from the way we describe it to others, based on the situation we find ourselves in. Thus, it can be good for us to consider the nuance of meaning in our own words when we confess, "I don't know how to pray," or something similar. We believe that as beings who were loved into creation, whenever we connect with the Divine, we are in prayer. So we can pray even when we don't feel that we can, or admit that we can, or share with others that we want to.

And so, we have multiple expressions of prayer—that are, until they're not, and that aren't, until they are. This resource will offer expressions of prayer that may be alive for you and not for others; however these apply to you, we hope you enjoy the warm companionship of Schrödinger's prayer.

Chapter 1

Prayer in Community

Most of this book addresses individual prayer practices and opportunities; but we feel that any book on prayer needs to at least consider the beauty, and even necessity, of corporate prayer, usually within the sacred space of church or chapel. This is not meant to suggest that "holy words" and "holy positions" used by "holy people" in "holy buildings" are somehow purer than everything else and, therefore, are more faithful expressions of faith. We simply consider that the community praying together in a specific location and time serves to sustain our prayers and places our individual efforts into a more holistic context.

One other point that we want to emphasize is almost all community worship is led by an individual (a priest, pastor, celebrant, leader, etc.; the title depends on the tradition of the community) or group of people, whose responsibility is to welcome the gathered people into worship and lead them through their time of prayer. This person or team is not more holy, or righteous, or closer to God than the rest of us mere mortals. He, she, or they are simply there to walk us all through the process of praying, so we don't need to be concerned about what comes next or not knowing how things are "supposed" to go. Relax! And follow their lead.

REGULAR WORSHIP

What Is It?

To best understand what regular worship is, we need to embrace the overall purpose. This practice takes us beyond ourselves and roots us in our communities. It helps us to celebrate being a part of the family of God, regardless of where our spiritual journey has taken us that week. It reminds us that every person we see is beloved of God (and invites us to shed our preconceived judgments, which may not be as charitable).

The purpose of communal worship is to support community and connection with one another. It gives us people whom we can approach when we need help, and offers our shoulders for those needing our assistance. Sharing the experience of worship helps us to focus on a bigger picture, where we embrace shared goals and vision of how to live the life that God has called us to.

The gift of a worshiping community also invites us to consider possibilities and perspectives that exceed our own. We strengthen ourselves in the faith, and our communities and neighborhoods are enhanced as we work to identify the values that inspire those who differ from us.

We are collectively refreshed through the word of God and invited into a place of prayer and praise. In communities that practice regular intercession, we vocalize our desire for the well-being of others (including those we may never have an opportunity to meet). The act of worshiping together demonstrates that as an interconnected community, we offer support when needed, we celebrate our joys when they occur, and we have a community to turn to when our spiritual journeys can feel off-track.

And, of course, in communal worship, we maintain a healthy appreciation that we are not coming together to be entertained or to receive accolades. As many memes remind us, if we don't enjoy worship, we may need to reflect on who we are worshiping.

We find that the rhythm of communal worship helps set a pattern for our days and weeks, and (in our liturgical traditions) can carry us through the ebbs and flows of life, through seasons that encompass the fullness of our human condition.

How Do I Do It?

Basically, show up! Being brave enough to enter the doors of a church that you are not familiar with takes courage and confidence, and it is a celebration of your genuine response to what God is whispering in your heart.

Trying out more than one church, or more than one denomination, is encouraged. This so-called "church shopping" is an opportunity to experience different styles of worship and faith community. There are many different expressions of church—in their theology, practice, service—as well as in the people who call that church "home." For example, if you're looking for a children's service, you should find somewhere that offers one. If the Holy Communion is a priority, you should seek out a church that makes it a weekly offering.

After worship, be honest with your assessment about the experience: if you knew what you were looking for in a church prior to the worship, consider if it met your needs and expectations. If they were not met, that may not be the place for you—but it does not mean that regular worship is not for you. There is a community for everyone; it can be helpful to be patient with the experience of finding the right one.

(At the same time, it may be helpful to ask yourself, "Why?" "Why did I not like the music? Why did the message not resonate with me? Why did I allow my likes and dislikes to distract me from what I needed to see or hear?" These are not easy questions, but they are quite often necessary.)

In looking for a faith community, it can also be beneficial to try a church a few times: on any given Sunday, a congregation may be experiencing an unusual time (such as grief over a members' death or celebration over a baptism), and such experiences are not indicative of the "norm."

When you are in the service of praise and prayer, allow yourself to be immersed within it. Listen to the prayers, hear the word of the Lord, celebrate with the people of God. The power of prayer and worship is a continual and global celebration; when we come together, we are participating in an offering to God in a manner that far exceeds what we could do on our own.

DAILY PRAYER

What Is It?

Most religious traditions encourage us to ground our days in intentional prayer. Many mainline traditions identify set prayers as part of the Daily Office (or Divine Office, or daily prayer). Most commonly, morning and evening prayers encapsulate this intention of commitment to prayer every day. These practices have been in place for millennia and supported by theologians in every age. When the medieval church began structuring prayer and collating prayers into books that were accessible by the masses, the Daily Offices were included with the intention that they could be prayed everywhere and by everyone; these prayers united the church well beyond the four walls of the buildings.

Scheduled prayers that bookend the day model a life that balances sacred and ordinary moments for Christians. Daily prayer provides a number of benefits to those who engage in the practice: it emphasizes unity of heart and mind; it connects people and communities to carry out the church's mission; it encourages a realistic assessment of the world around us; it situates prayer as foundational to Christian life; it serves as a constant daily reminder of Christ's presence; it highlights the gift of spiritual growth and direction; and it provides a necessary balance that nourishes prayer life in the good times and supports it in the dry spells.

Theologian Martin Thornton, who wrote extensively on the importance of daily prayer (from a mid-twentieth century Anglican perspective), describes prayer using an analogy of a fence: the weekly Eucharist is the sturdy fence posts, the Daily Offices are comparable to the cross beams that provide stability, and personal meditation (those daily casual conversations with God) make up the predominant slats to complete the fence. All the parts are interconnected and depend on each other in their unequal quantities to make the completed fence.[1]

Each expression of daily prayer will follow a basic structure: some form of gathering prayer, psalms, scriptural readings, possibly a canticle, a creed or affirmation of faith, intercessions, the Lord's Prayer, any additional collects or prayers of the day, and a blessing to end. Classic forms of daily prayer will follow a cycle of psalms that allows for all one hundred fifty to be read every month; and the Scriptures follow a lectionary.

1. See Thornton, *English Spirituality* or *Christian Proficiency*.

The Hymn "The Day Thou Gavest, Lord, Is Ended" (written by Rev. John Ellerton in 1870) celebrates the reality of the Divine Offices as a means to lean into Paul's invitation in 1 Thess 5:17 to "pray without ceasing." The hymn lyrics read thus:

> The day you gave us, Lord, has ended;
> the darkness falls at your behest.
> To you our morning hymns ascended;
> your praise shall hallow now our rest.
>
> We ask you that your church, unsleeping
> while earth rolls onward into light,
> Through all the world its watch is keeping,
> and never rests by day or night.
>
> As to each continent and island
> the dawn leads on another day,
> The voice of prayer is never silent,
> nor dies the strain of praise away.
>
> The sun, here having set, is waking
> your children under western skies,
> And hour by hour, as day is breaking,
> fresh hymns of thankful praise arise.
>
> So be it, Lord, your realm shall never,
> like earth's proud empires, pass away;
> But stand and grow and rule forever,
> till all creation owns your sway.[2]

How Do I Do It?

There are several ways to engage in daily prayer; the importance is to recognize that these prayers are intentional. They can be done individually or in congregational settings.

Some churches have a tradition of offering daily prayer (sometimes called the Divine Offices). If you are able to join a local group, it makes it easy. Alternatively, there are any number of churches around the world which offer daily prayer online.

2. This updated version cited in Evangelical Lutheran Church of America, *Evangelical Lutheran Worship*, hymn 569.

Even if, or maybe *especially* if, the church is a different tradition from your own, or if the whole experience of church is new for you, the language of their prayer may be outside of your experience or even seem foreign. This can be a challenge, but that's okay. Let it be a challenge. You are entering a new way of relating to God, to the church, to the world, and to yourself. It will be a journey, and since most of life does not go in a straight line, you can enjoy the twists and turns, trusting the promise that our prayers are heard, not because we are doing them "correctly" but because the One to whom we are praying is present.

Another option, if there is no daily prayer offered in your area or the online schedule doesn't work, you may make use of resources that can be easily found in most of the prayer books (and websites) of mainline churches.

SITUATIONAL PRAYER

What Is It?

These are structured prayer services that are intended for a particular occasion. They address a specific and unique situation. Some examples include funerals or weddings, vigils for peace, the Week of Prayer for Christian Unity, or the World Day of Prayer. Some communities will bless bicycles for commuters, backpacks for school children, tractors for farmers, or lobster boats for fishers.

Situational prayers can be a planned annual event or a response to something going on in the world. Whatever the impetus, they provide the rootedness and community that can be desired in the particular situation.

How Do I Do It?

In general, showing up is the main component. The folks leading these services are aware that not everyone attending is of that tradition or experience; some may never have been to that location or have only seen the rituals as presented on TV or in movies. (Hint: not all funerals have everyone dressed in all black with heels and hats and veils!)

If you are feeling uncomfortable, you can ask what to expect. Contact the host of the event to better understand what the service will entail, what practices might be expected, if there's a dress code, etc. A bit of foreknowledge can really help decrease stress.

Attending with someone else can also help to minimize any awkwardness; even if no one from your group has experience in this particular setting.

Finally: relax. These situational prayer services are unusual for everyone. The invitational information about the event may identify any expectations (such as a dress code for a wedding) or anticipated activities ("join us for a time of silent meditation"). Many events will have an order of service printed in some way, and most officiants will guide the service with helpful information along the way. If in doubt, you can look around the group to see if someone nearby appears to know what they're doing, and either ask them for help or simply copy their actions.

The following is an example.

LITURGY OF THE WOMEN

A portion of a service addressing the theme of intimate partner violence
Based on 1 Cor 13
Written in 2024 by Laura Marie Piotrowicz and Robin Newman[3]

For the Hannahs of the world, who know and speak their heart's desires to caring husbands and loving God, and who wait and see how God will bless them.

Love is patient;

For the Tabithas of the world, who use their skill to provide for the widows and those in need in their community;

Love is kind;

For the Lydias; whose financial stability could lead to a sense of superiority and acts of egotism, yet choose to use their means to promote the gospel alongside their friends

Love is not envious or boastful.

For the Abigails of the world, who use their diplomacy to de-escalate conflict and live in peace, in the name of God.

Love is not arrogant or rude.

For the Queen Vashtis of the world, who hold their dignity higher than the expectations of others.

3. Used with permission.

Love does not insist on its own way;

For the Ruths and Naomis, who have not experienced fairness in their lives, yet, who overcome adversity with dignity and grace.

Love is not irritable or resentful;

For the Deborahs of the world, who sit in justice, judging with righteousness and compassion.

Love does not rejoice in wrongdoing,

For the Eves, who are blamed for breakdowns in communication and relationship; for the Hagars, who are not afraid to speak truth to power.

Love rejoices in the truth.

For the Marys, like the God-bearer, who are supported by loving partners in the fulfillment of their mission, transformed by their faith in God.

Love bears all things, believes all things,

For the Miriams; whose faith exceeds the risks they face, and whose age is not a barrier to serving God.

Love hopes all things, endures all things.

For all the women in the Bible, those with names, those who are nameless, those who are forgotten by the editing of time. For all the women, who bear the love that God showers upon them.

Love never ends.

SEASONAL WORSHIP

What Is It?

This prayer moves with the rhythm of the church calendar and, at times, overlaps with the calendars of our secular society. These can include special offerings during liturgical seasons, such as midweek Lenten services or thematic focus, such as the season of creation. The big three times when these overlap are Thanksgiving, Christmas, and Easter.

Some churches may make light of the increased attendance for seasonal worshipers, sometimes dubbed "C & E Christians" (Christmas and Easter attendees). However, churches with a heart for ministry embrace the gift of those who have chosen to come into communal worship for those high festivals, as it indicates a potential to celebrate community and faith.

How Do I Do It?

Come to the church! It can be as simple as showing up. For some, this is as part of a family tradition (or sense of obligation); for others, it is part of nostalgia. It may emerge as a response from a deep longing that defies explanation. Whatever desire stirs within, it should be embraced.

Most churches will identify these seasonal, special services: look on their website or social media, read their outdoor signs, or call their offices. The goal of churches is to welcome folks in their spiritual journey; especially at deeply meaningful times of the year.

ACTS OF SERVICE

What Is It?

Prayer inspires us into action. Through prayer, we invoke the spirit to press us into service. A quote attributed to Pope Francis reminds us of our call to action: "You pray for the hungry, then you feed them. That's how prayer works."

Putting prayer into action extends beyond vocalized evangelism; these acts can have a purpose of welcoming and incorporating those new in the faith, supporting those at every stage of their faith journey, and establish meaningful partnerships with the wider community in ways that reflect the gospel call.

The process of discernment is integral when identifying ways to best take action within the community, for individuals, families, and the church as a collective. Honest consideration of interest and energy, a realistic assessment of resources, and intentional listening to the stories of those with whom the church engages allows for the best opportunity for fruitful ministry.

"Your vocation in life is where your greatest joy
meets the world's greatest need."

FREDERICK BUECHNER

How Do I Do It?

In Worship

Worship services themselves can be acts of service. Special Sundays may be identified as focal points to draw attention to issues and needs, such as collecting school supplies in summer or food bank collections at Thanksgiving.

We heard an anecdote of one church that adapted the fourth Sunday of each month to be a service Sunday; in place of the typical liturgical structure, the community would gather together with a call to worship, then spend time in small groups doing intentional acts of service (such as packing kits for folks in a seniors' residence or diaper kits for new mothers), and conclude with a closing prayer and benediction. These actions were determined by local needs identified by members who were engaged with the community at large.

In Community

Acts of service themselves can be prayerful, in the idea and the implementation. There are abundant opportunities to serve with the wider community, such as volunteering with food pantries, assisting in refugee resettlement, school tutoring, etc. Taking part in these activities is not meant to force others to be Christians, to join our churches, or conform to our way of thinking and doing. Rather, we do these actions because *we* are Christians and are responding to Jesus' invitation to care for the people in our midst who are experiencing need.

In Activism

Acts of activism can be a prayerful act, be they situational (such as protesting a war) or through ongoing advocacy efforts. Many church organizations invite attendance to rallies where injustice has been identified, such as holding placards at government offices to advocate for safe housing, or companioning with civil society organizations around global issues whose intersectionality affects us.

"Worship is advocacy and advocacy is worship."

Rev. Dionne Boissière, Chaplain of the Church Center for the United Nations

EXTEMPORANEOUS REQUESTS

What Is It?

There are times when we are asked to pray for someone. For those in leadership, often our title or the wearing of religious garb can attract a request for prayer. This is not limited to those of us who wear a clerical collar; in many places, someone who is known to be a member of a religious community can be asked to pray for someone.

How people ask for prayer will vary depending on the relationship and the circumstance; I've had beautiful moments at bedsides or before medical tests, requests for blessings before travel or school finals, chances to be surprised by the opportunity of prayer. I once had a gentleman stop me in the grocery store and proclaim enthusiastically, "Pastor! Pray for me!" I'd not met the man before and was merely trying to buy potatoes! (We went and prayed in the corner of the produce section. It was holy ground!)

How Do I Do It?

Firstly, acknowledge to yourself that someone asking for prayer is a special invitation into some form of trust and relationship—even the shortest encounters are meaningful.

Secondly, clarify the request when someone asks us to pray *for* them; "pray for me" could be a request for third-party prayers when someone cannot pray for themselves (such as during a medical procedure; unconsciousness is a good reason to request the assistance of the praying community). The request may arise from someone who refuses to pray for themselves, for whatever reason; this signifies a lack of connection with God and could lead to further conversation and understanding about their relationship with the Divine—and how prayer may aid in overcoming whatever barriers they feel exist. Another common cause when people ask for others to intercede for them is they feel they do not know how to pray, and so the request for prayers can also lead to an opportunity to learn. In these cases, I find the person is already praying but has not understood the conversation with God as such.

Honor the fact that some folks are asking for prayers in addition to their own prayers; and in these times, it is a gift to be trusted and welcomed into the community of people who pray, who raise petitions, requests, and thanksgivings from the broader church. This can be in a shared time of prayer or in collective commitment to prayer (such as a parish prayer list or the intercessions in the worship services).

Recognize that we can hear prayer requests through our own perspectives and perceptions. It is helpful to try and put away our own preconceived notions or preferences and just be present with people; we aren't trying to change someone else to our mode of thinking but to respond to an immediate plea in the most faithful way we can. (See also, chapter 14, "Prayer Gone Wrong.")

Finally, pray. The words of your mouth do not need to be eloquent or "perfect"; you are simply called to be present. The encounter desires an authentic spirituality, not a prophetic author. It is okay to say to God, in the presence of the person who has asked for prayers, that we do not have the words but we trust God to hear the stirrings of our souls and the whispers of our hearts. Many times, when words fail us, sharing the time by praying the Lord's Prayer can be deeply meaningful.

Chapter 2

The Classics

LITURGICAL RESOURCES

What Is It?

As Anglican and Lutheran, our traditions offer us a wealth of resources to match the seasons and cycles of the church calendar. The structure for many mainline churches is to follow prayers that have been written with a purpose of shared prayer over time and space. Liturgical resources provide the frameworks for daily prayers (Divine Office), prayers for times of day (the Hours), and seasonally appropriate foci. We benefit from the sharing of liturgical resources to enrich and enhance our common experience, as the increased body of resources offers not just more prayers but prayers addressing nuanced circumstances and situations that transcend denominational boundaries.

Our liturgical resources are designed to support and enhance our liturgy. While the word liturgy is often translated simply as "the work of the people," it is not restricted to our daily tasks. Liturgy is a collective holy act, a sacred effort done for the public good. Thus, it applies as the title to our shared worship but also to the collective ministrations that we do in the context of being the church. As the church, we are not a Sunday social club but the *ekklesia*, a diverse people gathered in unity because of God. As such, we benefit from the Greek roots of the word (*leitos* = public and *ergos* = working or ministering), which denote public service and collective worship as intricately intermingled. One cannot pray for the world without taking responsive action; one cannot do holy things without prayer.

It is helpful to remember that our liturgical resources are not intended to only be used in a certain building at a certain hour on a certain day, nor are they restricted to those who are ordained or licensed as liturgical leaders. Much of the prayers of the books are intended to guide worship that can enrich the lives of people wherever and whenever; from table graces to animal blessings, these resources assist all the faithful in recognizing and celebrating the divine communication in everyday life.

How Do I Do It?

Select a book: many mainline traditions have service books that can offer a variety of prayers. These tend to be unique in countries and denominations and, usually, the leadership of a worshiping community will be happy to discuss their resource and even lend a copy for you to explore.

The next step is as simple as opening the book! These resources are designed to be user-friendly; it may take some practice, but they lead through the ebb and flow of a healthy prayer experience. Many of these liturgical books include the psalter and a lectionary (calendar of Bible readings), which change day to day.

As you read the book and become more comfortable with the words on the page and the order in the resource, let the Spirit guide you as you pray the same prayers as many of God's people.

PRAYER BOOKS

What Is It?

There are countless books of prayers that can be found: these span millennia. They may be thematic, compilations, regionally focused, etc. They convey a wide breadth of theological standpoints, and so, it may take time to find a resource that speaks to your heart.

Note: we recognize the irony of including a section about prayer books in a prayer book! However, we both have invested a lot of funds and time in going through prayer resources, sometimes with great delight and sometimes elsewise. Just because a book has a certain number of stars in its rating or pops up as a recommendation on an online retailer doesn't necessarily mean that it will provide what you're looking for. This was part of our incentive to write this book as a buffet of options.

How Do I Do It?

Any bookstore or Christian library will have the ability to sell you a book of prayers. Some classic volumes may be available in free online repositories.

A starting point may be to discuss with your clergy or prayer group (or other trusted advisors), who can offer their perspectives and advice in terms of which book of prayers may be most helpful for you and your situation. (For example, a gentle daily devotional is different from a compilation of medieval prayers, which is different from a thematic collection, such as a focus on the psalms).

From there, the journey is yours to discover.

Don't give up after one effort; your first prayer book may not fulfill your expectations, or it may take you too far beyond your growing edge. If this happens, you may discuss this with a spiritual friend. We are all at different places at different times of our praying life. There may be the perfect book waiting for you just a couple of volumes further down the shelf.

PRAYING THE SCRIPTURES

What Is It?

This section articulates the nuance between reading, studying, and praying the Scriptures.

In *reading* the Scriptures, we are reading to learn the story. This is an exercise in comprehension, leading to awareness of the passage as a segment, the history of the book, the narrative arc, and the larger context of the scriptural passage itself. (Consider the classic questions of *who*, *what*, *when*, and *where*.)

In *studying* the Scriptures, we are exploring the context of the text, and examining connections between that context and ours, to discover insights into our own lives and situations. This is to increase depth of knowledge. A study group, class, or even a Bible commentary can be helpful for this. (This invites consideration of the classic questions *why* and *how*.)

In *praying* the Scriptures, we are simply spending time with them, open to what God might have to say to us in that moment. Having read and studied the passage, our headspace has the knowledge that will benefit. But here, we open our "heartspace" to the passage. We may hear a familiar story; we may notice something that we hadn't seen before; we may gain an insight or have an "aha!" moment. But the emphasis is on being present to the text, being present to ourselves, and being present to God.

There are times when we will not glean any new wisdom or discernment, and that is okay! This kind of prayer is not dependent on results or answers, which are the expected outcomes of reading and studying. The intentional time spent with the word of God is the prayer itself. It is time to be still, be open, and be grateful for the opportunity.

How Do I Do It?

Psalm 46:10 reminds us to "be still, and know that I am God." Praying the Scriptures takes us into this place.

The Bible can be prayed in an ordered way, by intending to reflect and pray on particular chapters and verses. We may take these prayers for a set amount of time or a specific number of verses. Or we may let the Spirit guide us.

Or we may simply open the Bible to a point that feels right, and see what God is going to reveal. Often, our Bibles may drop open to a familiar page and our eye is drawn to the message God desires for us to receive at that moment. (A friend tells a wonderful example of finding comfort in a hospital waiting room from an unexpected breeze flipping the pages of her Bible to the Scripture she benefited from seeing.)

However we start, the importance is *that* we start, with no expectation other than an intentional time with the word of God.

If you are someone who takes notes or doodles, it can be handy to have paper or your journal with you.

Beginning by being comfortable in body, try to be still in your heart and mind.

Thank God for the privilege of being able to read the Scriptures, of having literacy and access to the Bible, and opportunity of time and safety in which to engage.

Ask God to be present with you in this time of prayer.

Begin reading; allow yourself to stop whenever you need. Perhaps, your mind catches on a word or phrase that will encourage study. Perhaps, a feeling causes you to pause and reflect on a situation in your life.

Return to the words: this may be rereading the same portion over and over or continuing in the Scriptures. It may mean looking up other passages that you feel a connection to at this time.

Continue this slow pace through the Scriptures until you feel you are done (or it is time for you to go).

Thank God for what was revealed and/or for what remained hidden.

PRAYING THE HOURS/OFFICES

What Is It?

These structured prayers can be done individually or in a group and lead us on a series of transformation. These prayers are offered at established times (Hours) throughout the day to provide a framework of prayer for daily life. The Daily Office or Hours complement other worship services (such as the Eucharist) with a spiritual balance of prayer. They serve to collect the members of the Body of Christ into a community of people who pray, involved in different ways, with informed awareness of all spiritual believers and echoes of the call to care for self and family (1 Tim 3:4).

The Divine Office provides prayers for morning, noontime, evening, and night. These services have many names; matins or morning prayers, evensong or evening prayer, compline or night prayers. They evoke a rhythm of prayer to integrate all aspects of life. They are not long in duration but rich in meaning and steeped in tradition.

The discipline of praying at set times during the day has a long history of engaging all people in faith formation, and as such, many prayer books were written to serve, among other purposes, to simplify worship and to heighten the involvement of the full community. These prayers incorporate Scripture, daily prayer, intercessions, petitions, and the Lord's Prayer. They are rich in content, yet designed for every person to be able to follow and benefit from.

Modern prayer resources that provide daily offices can include prayer books and websites, podcasts and social media channels. Some include music while others are spoken. They are available in many languages and settings. The COVID-19 pandemic saw a number of churches and religious entities offering daily prayers in a variety of capacities, which served as a means to the Offices' return to common knowledge and use. Their ongoing popularity and outreach potential means this is a continuing offering of the broader church.

How Do I Do It?

Find a source for the prayer that speaks to you—in a community, as a family, as an individual. Be patient, as it may take some time and several attempts to feel comfortable with this pattern of prayer.

Commit to the time—to pray the Hours at the set time.

Pray. Daily.

Chapter 3

Contemplation

CONTEMPLATIVE PRAYER/MEDITATION

What Is It?

ALSO CALLED "CENTERING PRAYER," this practice is modeled on the practices of Desert Fathers and Mothers and invites an inward focus. It is not a form of isolationism but an intentional journey inward for a time. The Desert ancestors were not hermitting away to avoid the world but rather to demonstrate that they were not trapped by the world. They continued to interact with people on a regular basis; in sharing food and resources, in prayer and contemplation, in exchanging wisdom and theology. (Had they completely removed themselves from all human interaction, we would not have the abundant wisdom they have left for us.)

In a world where distractions are easy and focus isn't, this type of prayer can be a welcome refuge in the desire for some calmness. It rejects the concept of multitasking and instead provides a framework for deeper attention to the word of God, active in the world. This form of Christian meditation uses one word or phrase to maintain that focus. Your word will guide you to how God is present in your center. The focus may be easy or challenging; it may be comfortable or make us aware of unsettled feelings within.

How Do I Do It?

Sit comfortably, in a quiet place. Ensure that you have adequate time for this spiritual journey.

Be aware of your environment and rest your body. Tend to any physical needs so that you can be uninterrupted in the process. (Get a glass of water, silence your phone, etc.)

Take a few deep breaths and acknowledge your intention to be in love and faith with God and to seek God at your core. Be aware of God's presence with you.

Think of a word that expresses love; let it be present with you. Spend some time just hearing the word; you can say it aloud in different tones.

Reflect on the word. In what context do you normally hear this word? How do you say this word? Is it a normal part of your daily speech? What emotions does this word evoke in you?

If/as you become aware of anything else, acknowledge this but gently return to focus on God with the use of your word. You may want to write down other thoughts as a means to remember them afterwards.

When your heart has taken you as deep to your center as you wish, return to the wider, earthly focus. This may be through a well-known prayer such as the Lord's Prayer.

ICONS

What Is It?

Icons are an ages-old, intentional art form "created for the sole purpose of offering access, through the gate of the visible, to the mystery of the invisible."[1] These represent deep biblical and theological mysteries, using images of God or saints or heavenly beings as a tool for drawing the one who views them into deeper prayer. To aid in maintaining that focus, iconographers tend not to ascribe their names to the icon.

Icons are not art for art's sake; one does not draw an icon. Rather, the writing of an icon is a means through which the iconographer communicates access with the divinity in a medium that transcends beyond words. Icons are an artistic language, where every aspect of the icon (color, hand and eye directions, figures, angles, etc.) conveys a particular meaning. It is

1. Nouwen, *Behold*, 23.

not essential to fully understand or articulate these meanings as you pray with icons, but it can be helpful to understand how they influence your attention and prayer. Meanings can be ascertained later, in research.

As icons often correlate to scriptural passages, they serve both to enhance and to be enhanced by the written word in a beautiful symbiotic relationship. You aren't required to know which passage is being referenced to appreciate praying over it. Not unlike stained glass windows, this art form is a visual immersion into the history and tradition of the Christian community.

How Do I Do It?

As with all practices, undertaking a new practice will take time and can benefit from engaging a guide. With icons, such guides can aid in the understanding of history and purpose of each icon. As unique colors, shapes, and influences carry significant meanings, such resources can greatly assist in the process. Many Orthodox churches can offer guidance from their priests. These guides may stay with you throughout your prayer, or offer their guidance and leave you to ponder the icon(s) alone with God.

Choose an icon that attracts you. You do not need to understand the attraction, but ask God to direct you to the image that will deepen your prayer.

Look at the icon: gaze into it, seeing it not as an impressive piece of artwork but as a revelation of the divine message. Meditate on the art in the same way you would meditate on the Scriptures in *lectio divina*, or contemplate on a holy word in centering prayer. How is God speaking to you in this icon? How is God inviting you deeper within through this icon?

Continuing to look at the icon, reflect on your personal experience with it. What is God saying to you through this icon? What message is God giving to you? How do you feel about your place in the world as a result of this icon?

Going deeper, consider how this icon will inspire you to respond. What ministry is God calling you to? What prayers are being stirred in your heart? What words or ideas come to mind, what people are you remembering? Journaling here can be helpful.

Finally, rest in the presence of the icon. Be gentle and patient with yourself, regardless of your meditations and reflections; the rest may be what God was calling you to today. Icons are not meant as to-do list generators but as spiritual aids.

Give thanks to God for the time and space of this experience.

THE EXAMEN

What Is It?

This is a teaching from the practices of Ignatius of Loyola, a sixteenth-century priest and theologian and one of the founders of the Society of Jesus (the Jesuit tradition). His spirituality was grounded in the truth of God's presence to all of us, in every aspect of our lives. Ignatian prayer practices aspire to help people better recognize this personal connection with God that will lead to intentional discernment of God's call, acts of service, and deeper prayer.

The Ignatian exercises specifically invite a daily reflection on the events of the day. Ignatius followed that there are two main reactions to pay particular attention to: consolations (moments of inexplicable joy, a connection to God) and desolations (moments of dis-ease or disconnect).

Within the exercises, the Examen is based on our being truthful with ourselves and with God, practicing a desire for spiritual growth, and being increasingly aware of God's work in the ordinary moments of our lives. It is a practice of self-reflection in order to have a better understanding of ourselves and our place in the world, hoping that what we do is of benefit to all of God's world. It is a prayer where we review the day, speaking to Jesus as we would our closest friend.

How Do I Do It?

Find a quiet spot, and be comfortable.

Consider the activities of the day, as though describing to God what happened, the facts and the emotions. This can help to clarify the daily events or demonstrate patterns from the busyness of daily living.

Seek consolation: ask God to remind you of today's moments of gratitude. What was today's best moment? What made it so good? When did you give and receive the most love today?

Seek desolation: ask God to reveal your most difficult moment of the day. What words and actions made this moment so difficult? Sit with your feelings without aiming to change them.

Express gratitude: recognize that every moment is an opportunity to learn, and thank God for the people and situations in your day. Gratitude could be for something as simple as a good cup of coffee or as complex as the completion of a long-term task.

Discern one aspect of the day that is staying with you in your reflections. Pray about that reality, whether or not you understand what God is saying to you through this part of your day.

Identify your hopes for tomorrow—not long-range planning or the daily to-do list, but a careful consideration of how God may be revealed in the coming day. This is a time to honor any concerns and excitements, any prayer requests, and to ask for awareness of God accompanying you through whatever life will hold.

Thank God for the time of intimate connection.

You can share your reflections with a trusted friend, a spiritual director, or in a journal. These reflections may help to reveal patterns in your life over time.

Chapter 4

Movement

DANCE

What Is It?

DANCE ALLOWS MOVEMENT TO encompass the act of prayer in ways that words cannot. This intentional activity adopts incarnational theology, empowering the dancer to pray with body as well as with mind.

This is not just movement but choreography; just as memorizing words of a prayer, the motions of the dance are careful and articulated to elicit a specific reaction.

For those who are kinesthetic learners, or those whose primary means of communication is not through words, dance can provide a structured and practiced expression of spirit.

Dance as prayer can be done individually or with others; it can be representative or abstract. It may be intended to be performative (as liturgical dance) or as private expression. It is a physical manifestation of a desire of the soul, expressing gratitude, reverence, and honor to God, as a means of spiritual journeying.

Dance provides an ages-old outlet for connection with God and is seen throughout the Bible in prayerful ways:

- As a counter to mourning, or a signifier that the time of lament has passed: the familiar "a time for everything" passage presents these as direct opposites (Eccl 3:4b: "A time to mourn, and a time to dance");

In Luke 7:32, Jesus notes that the invitation to pray has been given, yet many did not take it ("We played the flute for you, and you did not dance"); the people describe their grief at the loss of the temple (Lam 5:15: "The joy of our hearts has ceased; our dancing has been turned to mourning").

- As a faithful act of celebratory thanksgiving: Miriam leads a dance of gratitude for the safe escape from Egypt in Exod 15 ("Then the prophet Miriam, Aaron's sister, took a tambourine in her hand; and all the women went out after her with tambourines and with dancing"); when David brings the Ark of the Lord to the city of David (2 Sam 6:14a: "David danced before the Lord with all his might"); the joyous father celebrates the return of the prodigal son in the Gospels (Luke 15:25: "Now his elder son was in the field, and as he came and approached the house, he heard music and dancing"); Jer 31:4 includes dancing as part of the celebration when the exiles of Israel return ("Again you shall adorn yourself with your tambourines and go forth in the dance of the merrymakers").
- As a prayer of celebration that defies remaining still: the psalms addressing praise, often include dance; Ps 30:11 at the dedication of the temple, Ps 149:3, and Ps 150:4 are hymns of praise; intending nothing more than to praise God, they include dance as a means of communicating that emotion and intention.
- As an oblation: the indication of music (of instruments and voice, being intentionally offered as an oblation) bring forth the imagery of dancing (while they do not directly proclaim it): Psalm 68:25 and 40:3, 71:23, 105:2—the list embraces the presence of prayerful joy.

How Do I Do It?

Dance!

Engage with someone who actively participates in prayerful dance or dance as prayer.

Try a number of practices, with actions that match the words of familiar prayers or with a group of liturgical dancers.

Explore the ways that your body responds to certain movements; this manner of praying is not constant!

Be open to the Spirit guiding you through the process of learning, and through the ways your body responds to the dances you pray.

Ensure you are not engaging in performative religion (where the focus is on you or the moves themselves), but keep your heart open to the dance as a fluid communication with the Divine.

It may be helpful to debrief and unpack prayer dances with your instructors or a spiritual director.

MOVEMENT

What Is It?

Both of us can share anecdotes of holy moments that surround movement: the simple movement of the body, without choreography or conduction. We see these as expressions of prayer, as they have remained with us as divine teachings years later. We share them here.

When I was a student intern, the parish I was placed in (for a very short amount of time) had engaged in refugee resettlement. We were blessed to be the Canadian home to a mother and her children. Her youngest child was deaf from birth, due to traumas from the refugee experience. One day, as the energetic processional music was playing, he shifted slightly away from his mothers' side, and we saw him making subtle bouncing movements, seemingly in time to the music. This continued throughout the hymn, increasing in movement as he was feeling the vibrations of the music. The priest recognized that this child felt safe and was expressing a physical response to the music, and invited the musician to continue playing after the end of the hymn. We watched as this young child began swaying and dancing, moving into the aisle even; and we danced with him. There were no coordinated steps; we didn't know what verse we were singing; we didn't know how long it would last, but the Spirit had clearly been active in him, and he knew he was on holy ground. We all benefited from the experience of seeing joy flow through this child of God. After the impromptu dance party was over, the priest merely announced that we had all witnessed, and participated in, the living gospel for the day.

When singing with an ecumenical choir, we once did a piece written by a South African composer. After one performance, we learned that some attendees at the concert had South African roots. Our conductor sought them out and asked them for feedback in the interest of providing a deeper appreciation for and, in the future, a more authentic presentation of the piece. The women were generous and gracious in their feedback, saying that the choir had sung the sounds accurately; however, they said, "At home, we're not singing unless we're moving." Swaying, clapping, turning, foot or hand movements—these are all an integral part of the experience of singing. Movement of the body is an embodiment of the music and, therefore, an embodiment of the prayer that music is.

How Do I Do It?

Our bodies are designed for movement, and as such, our prayers can be augmented by simple movement. Though both of our examples are rooted in music, this movement is not restricted to life's soundtrack; our examples merely reflect that music is a great and natural basis for movement. However, any movement that we make in response to the Spirit can be prayer, be it fidgeting, dancing, even just contracting muscles—our bodies respond to how God is speaking to us in that moment. Part of this as a spiritual practice is to recognize that not all movement is prayerful, but any movement has the potential to be prayerful. In opening our hearts and minds to the possibility, we can engage in prayerful movement (even if we can't articulate it with words).

NEIGHBORHOOD PRAYER WALKING

What Is It?

This form of intercessory prayer involves a spiritual and physical journey to a place of prayerful concern: the home neighborhood. It is a time to connect our prayerful hearts to the physical space that we inhabit. By being intentionally mindful while in that space, we become more and differently observant to that space, what is going on around it, and with the people involved.

It can be as simple as praying when walking an established route or familiar pathways; it can be intentionally unintentional, meandering wherever the spirit (and your feet!) lead. The prayers are extemporaneous, as you allow your mind to focus on whatever is present in the community that day.

Planned neighborhood prayer walking can be a scheduled route around the neighborhood, going between landmark places (i.e., the fire hall to the library to the church); though a plan should not interfere if the Spirit is guiding you in an unexpected direction. On a smaller scale (or on a day of inclement weather), such a walk could take place in one location (i.e., a church) and focus on the various places and spaces within (such as the windows or the layout of architecture).

How Do I Do It?

Set some time, and go for a walk: not as a means of getting from one point to another but to know the place and people more deeply. As you pass various buildings and people, hold them up before God. Be conscious of the use of land in the area and if it aligns with God's vision of creation. Pray for each space, its purpose and people. For example, when passing a fire station, you could pray for first responders, fire fighters, dispatchers, victims of fire. If passing a child's bike on the sidewalk, pray for healthy children, active families, safety, community.

Notice what is consistent, what is different, what feels comfortable, what catches your attention. Be aware of your connection with each place and with the people who live and work there. How can you see the presence of Jesus in these places?

Pay attention to the presence of nature: hear the birds, touch the grass, smell the earth. Be mindful of the presence of the divine in the ongoing revelation through creation.

At the end of your walk, thank God for revealing the prayerful opportunities in your neighborhood. Reflect on what it means to you to see God in these places. What helped you to concentrate on God? What was distracting? Is God speaking a particular prayer into your heart? Does your intentional focus on this place as belonging to God change how you interact with it? Reflect on the way your body feels: do your feet hurt, is your back sore, do you feel energized by the increased oxygen and blood flow?

WALKING THE LABYRINTH

What Is It?

This practice involves an ancient pathway of contemplation and meditation: a labyrinth is a walking prayer. The journey follows a path that will guide into and out from the center. The labyrinth is different from a maze, as there is no possibility of getting lost or stuck or needing to start over. The journey is always leading through turns and pathways that are safely going to and from the center; there are no dead ends or traps. This is a comforting reality reflective of our journey with God. Since there is no need to follow or find the "right path," we can simply allow our feet to go forward and let our mind and heart rest in the presence of God on the way. In this way, the labyrinth walk becomes a journey of discernment.

While a physical labyrinth is required, it can be a walking space (frequently modeled on the labyrinth found in the floor of the Chartres Cathedral, many spaces have labyrinths either constructed into their floor, on a canvas mat, or in hedges outdoors), or it can also be a finger labyrinth, where the pattern is drawn on paper, sewn/quilted into fabric, or molded of fired clay or other material.

Meeting people along the way is not abnormal; in fact, it can enhance the journey. The acts of stepping aside or passing one another can be indicative of life's journey. So, too, is walking in the same direction as someone else; they may be ahead of us or behind us, and we may not always journey at the same pace. There can be need for discussion as one person advances past another while remaining on the shared pathway.

Pauses are also common during a labyrinth prayer; when moments of enlightenment or concern arise, it can be healthy and helpful to pause where you are to fully acknowledge and consider the learning to be had. Likewise, being cognizant of the increase and decrease of your speed while you journey through a labyrinth experience can also be revelatory.

How Do I Do It?

Pause at the start of the labyrinth. Try to calm your mind, to be fully present to the experience.

Enter into the labyrinth with trust and expectation.

Go into the space with intention: you can begin this journey seeking direction on a particular issue (keeping one topic or discernment issue in mind), or you can leave your heart open.

As you journey, ask yourself questions, such as, what am I bringing with me? What do I wish to leave at the center? Who or what is causing me to alter my path? What is my center? What am I hoping to receive? What grace do I seek?

Leave the labyrinth with gratitude and thanksgiving.

After your time in the labyrinth, try to spend some time in reflection. Ask yourself, what have I experienced? What has become clearer? What questions have arisen? What am I taking with me? How can I look for God's presence in my other journeys? You may wish to journal or discuss the experience with a spiritual director.

YOGA

What Is It?

Yoga[1] is, in origin, a classical Indian Hindu spiritual practice that attempts, through assuming prescribed physical positions, controlled breathing, and meditation, to assist the practitioner to clear the mind and gain personal spiritual insights. It is now a worldwide phenomenon, with practitioners from a variety of religions and non-religious traditions, who use yoga as everything from a simple exercise routine to an attempt to achieve oneness with the universal spirit.

In talking with yoga practitioners, they have repeatedly stated that the practice is not just about "positions" or "postures." We make this same statement for Christian prayer. It's not about assuming a correct position; we can pray anytime, anywhere, and in any pose. In the same way, both yoga and Christian prayer are not just about managing the rate of our breathing; they are about awareness.

That being said, human beings are physical creatures who inhabit space and move through time, and so, our bodies are a primary way that Christians engage in prayer. This allows us to pay attention to our position, our movement, our stillness. We can be intentional about breathing our prayer in and out. We can engage in practices that call us to our physicality, remembering and celebrating that "the word became flesh and lived among us" (John 1:14).

How Do I Do It?

There are websites, books, and classes that can teach you different positions and different approaches to this practice. Doing some intelligent research will help greatly.

Prepare your space (mats, pillows, lighting, phone on silent mode, etc.).

1. See "Interfaith Issues" in the introduction.

You might choose a focus for your prayer (a need, a situation, a fear, a joy, etc.), or you may allow yourself simply to *be* in the presence of God.

Begin with some warm-up positions (yoga practitioners call these *asanas*). You may sit with legs crossed (the *suhkasana*), stand with arms extended to the ceiling/sky and palms joined together (the *urdhva hastasana*), lie flat on your back with palms pointing upward (the *savasana*). As you progress, you may try more advanced positions (see below for some resources).

Note: do not do anything that causes discomfort or may result in injury. This is not about pushing past limitations; this is about embodied prayer.

Close your eyes and breathe gently.

When it seems appropriate, offer your prayer. Do it slowly, in concert with your breaths. A simple, repetitive prayer can work very well, such as, "Jesus Christ" as you inhale, "have mercy on me" as you exhale.

Some versions of yoga change positions every four to ten breaths, while others hold the same position for a more extended time. There is no right or wrong way; do what works for you.

As you do your cool down, give thanks for this time of prayer.

PRAYER BEADS

What Is It?

This is a set of prayer beads that guide repetitive prayers. Based in a centuries-old Orthodox tradition, this devotional aid can be used individually or in groups. Depending on the prayers chosen, they can reflect the seasons of the church, a particular devotional focus, or as a daily resource.

Not merely "prayerful fidgeting," praying with beads is a directed course of prayer. These are intended to calm the person praying, as the tactile nature of the prayer invites us to slow down, remove ourselves from distractions, and be mindful of the richness of the prayers. The symbolism of the rosary is intentional as it guides both our conscious and subconscious selves into the deeper mystery.

There are several resources to consider the prayers themselves, including liturgical texts and prayer books. Many purchased rosaries will include a few samples of such devotions.

The beads themselves consist of a cross and thirty-three beads (symbolizing the thirty-three years of Jesus' life). There are twenty-eight smaller beads and five larger beads. The smaller beads and four of the large beads form a circle, with the final large bead and cross serving as an entry and exit to the cycle.

Entering into this cycle of prayers begins with the cross, as the praying person welcomes the presence of God.

The next bead is the invitatory bead, which invites the person into the holy space.

The next bead, one of the four of the circle, is called a cruciform bead. The cruciforms are each divided by seven of the smaller beads (called "weeks" and symbolic of the days of creation). In the circle, they form a cross pattern, hence the title "cruciform."

The cycle of the loop (the twenty-eight weeks and four cruciforms) can be prayed once or repeated as desired; the act of praying continues as long as you would like. Once you feel it is time to return to the space beyond the prescribed prayers, you simply complete the cycle you are in, and leave the prayer time by the invitatory and cross.

Prayer beads can be purchased or made; some have beads of wood or metal or plastic; others have beads made of knots in a continuous twine; it can be a craft for confirmation class or even drawn on paper and traced with a finger. The substance for the device is not important; the rhythm of prayers remains the focus.

How Do I Do It?

One example of a cycle of prayers, by bead, follows:

- *The Cross*: In the name of God, Father, Son, and Holy Spirit. Amen.
- *Entering (the invitatory bead)*: O God, make speed to save me; O Lord, make haste to help me. Glory to the Father, and to the Son, and to the Holy Spirit: as it was in the beginning, is now, and will be forever. Amen.
- *The Cruciforms*: Holy God, Holy Almighty, Holy Immortal One, have mercy upon me.
- *The Weeks*: Lord Jesus Christ, Son of God, have mercy on me, a sinner.
- *Exiting (the invitatory bead)*: The Lord's Prayer.
- *The Cross*: I bless the Lord, in the name of Christ.

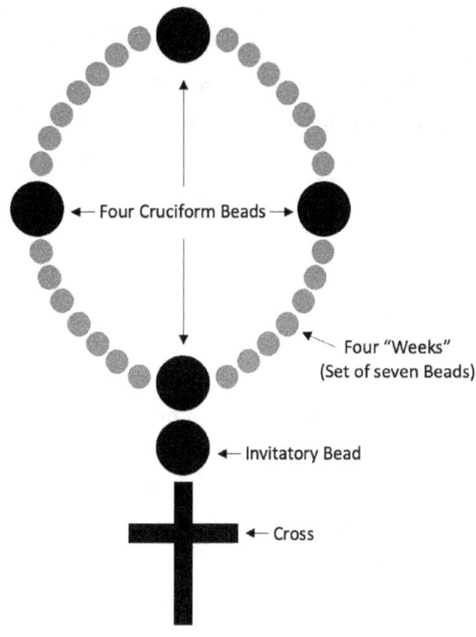

EXERCISE

What Is It?

Different from just the physical benefits of exercise, this is an intentional time to engage in prayer while undertaking particular movement. This exercise can be cardiovascular, isometrics, weight lifting, whatever. A simple walk is an exercise that can be prayerful. This is not spontaneous movement (as described above). Instead, prayerful exercising enables a distancing from distractions or interruptions that may be found in other venues where prayer exists; it also opens up the possibility of our prayer taking a different route than what we had planned.

Our physical movement will increase the flow of blood through our veins, thereby reminding us of the life force that our faith provides. As the oxygen increases in our lungs, we consider the breath of God that gives all life. The act of exercising may result in our feeling an increase in physical energy and, thus, feeling more inspired into spiritual exercising (i.e., prayer). You generally won't fall asleep during prayer time when walking!

How Do I Do It?

Literally, place one foot in front of the other, or raise your arms above your head, or stretch your muscles in coordinated and known movements. Whatever your preferred form of exercise, be intentional about inviting God to be present at that time in those movements.

If you find yourself frustrated at work, your walk to the water cooler could be a prayerful pathway towards God's gift of patience. If you are feeling distressed by the nightly news, stretch your body in ways that feel life-giving (while turning off the life-depleting news). There are ways that our seemingly little actions can actively counter the harshness of the world around us. Likewise, we have seen people react with movement when they are celebrating: raising arms in joy, doing a literal "happy dance" when receiving good news, etc. These movements can also be used as times of prayer.

We recognize that the ability to disconnect from whatever is ailing us, or to pause the rhythm of our day to celebrate what has filled us with joy, is a privilege. There are many for whom the ebb and flow of life does not permit these luxuries. Thus, we recognize the potential for spiritual growth by staying in the discomfort and finding ways to take action against the injustices of the world. This further encourages us to exercise the right to do what is right.

In physical exercise, growth happens just beyond the comfort zone (muscular strength needs to be challenged), which leads to a mantra of "be comfortable with being uncomfortable." This is also a spiritual reality. We encourage those engaging in prayer to commit to staying with the prayer until the matter touching your heart is resolved.

Chapter 5

Creative Appreciation (Taking in the Mystery)

VISUAL ART PRAYER (*ARS DIVINA*)

What Is It?

THIS CONTEMPLATIVE PROCESS FOLLOWS a similar theme as *lectio divina* (see chapter 9), but with a focus on a piece of visual art. This can be at a gallery, in a book, on your fridge as a child's gift. The art can be any style or medium, so long as it is a visual artwork. You will spend time (a minimum of ten minutes) considering deeper awareness of God's revelation through the art.

This practice differs from art appreciation as the focus is not on the art itself; though, undoubtedly, the brush strokes, color choices, or fabric selections are important. To consider this as prayer, we pay attention to the way that God is speaking through the art. The focus then does not lie on the artist's person or their other works, nor does the prayer depend on the intention of the art piece. The art is a vehicle for connection with the divine through meditation.

How Do I Do It?

Find a comfortable space where you can sit and easily view the artwork. Establish a way to share your insights (journaling, discussing with a companion, etc.). If necessary, find a way to maintain your focus—in a busy gallery, putting on quiet music through earphones can help to enhance the focus—and thereby help prevent getting caught up in other visitor's conversations or other distractions. Such music, however, should enhance the experience, not compete with it.

Take time to consider the artwork in silence.

Describe what you see without interpretation. A painting of a woman with an apple, for example, is a woman with an apple.

Consider the artwork more. What meaning do you interpret from the image? (The woman with the apple, for example, may remind you of Eve, and you may interpret if she is in Eden or a backyard. Has she yet eaten the fruit?) We apply much of our own understanding of the world into our interpretation of art.

Spend more time viewing the art. Looking beyond your personal interpretation, consider additional aspects of the artwork. What draws your attention? What feelings are stirred up within you? Where is your eye drawn to? Is that significant? What does this image make you think about? What Scripture passage does this bring to mind? How is God using this image to convey a message to you about your own journey?

If time allows, continue to consider the artwork, focusing on the aspects and spaces that you have not spent time on before. What is there that you haven't seen? Is this reflective of some aspect in your life you're avoiding? What lessons might be learned, this day or in the future, from this alternate focus?

As you are ready to move away from the exercise, thank God for the time to engage through the art. Thank God for the artist and their gift. Thank God for the learnings of the experience, and pray for those issues that have become known to you during this process.

MUSIC AS PRAYER

This section deals with listening to music. See the next chapter for thoughts on writing or composing music.

What Is It?

Music is found throughout the Bible. It is sung; it is played; it is chanted. God's people are invited (and sometimes even commanded) to make music, to listen to music, to learn music, to compose music, and even to pray music, both individually and with each other. The earliest verse of Scripture we have in the Bible is a song! (Exodus 15:21: "And Miriam sang to them: 'Sing to the Lord, for he has triumphed gloriously; horse and rider he has thrown into the sea.'")

Music points us to the good, the true, and the beautiful.

We might hear the "good" in a virtuoso performance, in a five-year-old singing "Happy Birthday," in a recording of a once in a lifetime partnership in front of a live audience, in a song that reminds us of what is real in our world, in joining our voice to others as we sing a song of praise or a choral work.

We can hear the "true" in the purity of a single flute, in lyrics that proclaim faith, in the demands or frustration of a protest song, or in the anger of a rap musician.

We may experience the "beautiful" in a simple song or a complex symphony, in contemplative pieces or intricate jazz riffs, in a classic hymn or a tune we just made up ourselves, or even in praying through the tears as we sing the words of a departed loved one's favorite piece.

Music can support our prayer; it can inspire our prayer, and it can even be our prayer. As Augustine is often quoted as saying, "[The one] who sings prays twice."[1]

Music is a medium for engaging in prayer, whether by singing, reading of the words, or even humming along with a recording while listening to the delicate dance of the notes and rhythm. In this way, music represents a relationship that is a conduit of holiness.

Music takes us to the good, the true, and the beautiful. Music is prayer.

How Do I Do It?

There are a number of ways to engage with music as prayer:

1. *Catechism of the Catholic Church*, 299.

Option One

Consider the lyrics of a song or hymn. Do this without the accompanying music to engage with the content as a prayer. How is God speaking to you through the lyrics? How do they relate to your life? What is the attraction to these words?

If the lyrics are based on Scripture, consider how they vary from the original text in your Bible. Has the message changed? Is there nuance to enhance or detract from the biblical passage? What might God be saying to you through the differences?

Option Two

Find a melody that resonates with your heart. Does the melody remind you of an event or a loved one? Is it particular to a season? How does the tune speak to you without any words? Was the tune written to accompany a particular set of lyrics or purpose, and if so, is that important to you?

Use this music as a background focus for your prayer time. Allow it to become a trigger for prayer, so that your spirit enters into prayer whenever you hear it.

Option Three

Pick a song to listen to with intentionality. Try to be fully present to the song. Do the lyrics connect with the tune? If the lyrics were sung to a different tune, or different lyrics to the same tune, would that change your feeling towards the sacred nature of the song?

How is your body reacting? What conversations are you having with God through the song? What feelings does the music inspire in you or free you to experience? Does it draw you deeper into your true self? Or does it draw you out of yourself and into the presence of the God who is with you and with all?

Repeat the song as much as you like.

FAITH ON FILM/THE SACRED ON STAGE

What Is It?

Basically, this form of prayer invites us to reflect theologically on performances we view, be they films or plays. The viewer intentionally considers how to see beyond the immediate presentation and understand aspects of God's presence and work in the film or play as invitations to hear God's voice in our lives.

There are numerous ways to reflect theologically, and several wonderful models have been developed by groups that focus on spiritual development.

Many communities offer groups that will gather for film viewing and discussion or reading books that take a group through guided discussion questions about particular films and plays. While there are also countless resources that offer insights of this practice, we encourage you to consider engaging in these reflections on your own prior to a ready-made analysis.

How Do I Do It?

Select a film or play to consider. It does not need to be a religious film/play.

Ask God to guide your journey, to see the messages of the film that are meaningful for where you are in your spiritual journey.

Watch the movie/play! (Snacks may be encouraged, depending on the venue.)

Keep a notebook with you, to jot down things that catch your attention so that you can revisit them after the film or play is over. If it's a film at home, try not to pause it but make note of being fully present to the entirety of the storyline.

After the film/play, take some time for intentional reflection. The following questions may be answered in order, or you may find answers popping up as you reflect:

- Consider how the film or play made you feel; what memories did it evoke in you?
- Identify what characters or situations struck a chord with you. How did you connect to the characters or actions, and why?

- What were the belief structures or morals that the film or play presented and embraced? Do you agree with them? Disagree? To what extent? And why?
- What aspects of the setting reminded you of your current cultural context? Does that make a difference in how you understood the theme of the film /play?
- What aspects of your faith tradition or practice did you notice in the film/play? Did you feel they were adequately and accurately portrayed?
- How was God present for you in the film/play?
- What messages or lessons might you glean from the film/play?
- How will you allow this film/play to influence your faith journey?

You can spend as much or as little time in reflection as you are comfortable. If you are with a group, you may share as much or as little as you are comfortable, though everyone in the group should be given adequate time and space to share without interruption.

Thank God for the time to seek the divine presence in the midst of a recreation activity.

Some people enjoy revisiting the film or play (in whole or in specific parts) after their initial time of reflection to see if the awareness of their reflection deepens or shifts.

PRAYER GARDENS

What Is It?

Any garden can be a prayer garden. It is an intentionally constructed and maintained space that elicits prayer from within us. For some, this is a space that has been previously cultivated; for others, it is a space that they will create. (Therefore, we place prayer gardens at the end of chapter 5, as the two options under "How Do I Do It?" bridge the creative space between appreciative and generative prayers.)

There are many aspects of a prayer garden: water, shade, a gentle or soft feeling, plants, and more. There may be a meandering path, perhaps statues of saints or animals that mark the journey. A pergola or bench may indicate a place for rest; additions like lights or decorations or topiaries may create a focus space for reflection. The garden does not need to have a set path through it; it may be simply a small corner of a yard or a section of city balcony that has been dedicated for the purpose. The garden may have a wilderness feeling or a cultured aesthetic; it may focus on greenery, water, rocks, or be overrun with colorful flowers.

Whatever the garden looks like, it is a place of peace and sanctuary in which to breathe, pray, meditate, and generally reconnect with God through immersion in a living environment. As naturalist Henry David Thoreau said, "The question is not what you look at, but what you see."[2]

A prayer garden can also be a place where the relationship with the space, through maintenance, becomes the prayer itself. A garden (any garden) can offer us reflection on ourselves; a garden is always a work in progress; it offers boundless opportunities to grow; there's usually benefit (and at times need) to do some weeding; and generally, there are seeds full of potential, waiting below the surface for the opportune time.

How Do I Do It?

Option One: Appreciation

If your goal is to visit a prayer garden, then the doing is in the presence. Recognize the space as holy, as a means to re-ground yourself in the created world that God has loved and called into being.

Allow yourself to be immersed in the space, letting go of the troubles of the world.

If you are seeking peace in reading a book or a prayer service, this is an ideal setting.

Make a physical connection with the garden by touching a flower or walking with bare feet to feel the grass.

Recognize the connections through other senses: the unique aromas, the sounds of the birds or insects, etc.

Breathe deeply.

Give thanks for the space and the time, for the people whose efforts have allowed this space to be.

Commit to keeping some of this garden peace with you in your heart and mind when you leave the garden.

2. Thoreau, "Journal 2: Chapter 7," 373.

Option Two: Construction

If your goal is to create or maintain a prayer garden, then the focus amplifies what is also in the visiting.

Identify the space with intention.

Create a plan for the prayer garden.

Establish the garden; getting your hands dirty (metaphorically and literally).

Remove the overgrowth, rocks, or dead remains from years past—anything that would hinder new life.

Tend the soil, ensuring a healthy foundation for growth to happen.

Pause to give thanks for the potential: in the garden, in your life, and in the lives of others that you know and love.

Realize the plans for your garden: plant the greenery, mark any pathways, adorn with decorations.

Once the garden is created, maintain it as a prayerful experience; reflect on what weeds you can remove from your spiritual journey as you pluck those dandelions; as you water, you can recognize areas of your soul that are thirsting for justice; consider what aspects of your ministry might benefit from some fertilizing when you see plants that just aren't thriving. Gardens can teach us much about ourselves when we engage.

Visit your garden; celebrate it as the haven you intended it to be. If you are so inclined, you can share this space with others.

Chapter 6

Creative or Generative Prayer

As created beings, within the realm of all creation, we are also creators. God has blessed us with creativity and filled us with inspiration in order that we can create. As we live in the spirit and are surrounded by countless expressions of creation, our creative juices are meant to be explored and played with. Use of color, language, space, pattern, sound—however we engage our senses—is a way to celebrate that we are co-creators with our Creator.

As we create, we are making things to be. To generate something is to create it.

A world of similarity will hamper creativity; if we all lived in monochromatic blocks, we could only imagine monochromatic blocks. However, God has given us the enormity of creation, some of which we are just discovering, other parts will be revealed only to future generations.

The outcome of our creating could be abstract or concrete, permanent or temporary, using anything as a medium (and using multiple media for some!). Wood, paint, rocks, sea glass, cake decorating . . . the possibilities are endless. We offer just a few ideas of using our creativity as prayerful intention, as this chapter invites us to confidently dive deeper into our imaginations in the same way that we encourage children to develop their creativity through play. When something is created or generated, it is tapping into that same energy that blessed all of creation from the Genesis moment. May we honor that first beginning with our own confidence to create.

KNITTING/YARN CRAFT

What Is It?

Using yarns or wools, the interconnection of strings into a cohesive unit as a fabric or textile, is an art form that has been used for centuries and across cultures. These crafted materials can be shawls, scarves, sweaters, mittens . . . just about anything can be created with a variety of textures, patterns, and colors. This can follow any manner of creative practice—knitting or looming or crocheting or any other way to weave.

What will make an article of yarn craft into a spiritual practice is the intention behind it: prayer. When each stitch is a prayer, a lap quilt becomes a prayer shawl. The article itself becomes an opportunity for the creator to pray; it also then infuses prayer into the stitches. Thus woven, with every stitch a prayer, the garment can be blessed within the broader worshiping community and then distributed to those experiencing need. This can be people who are in hospital or care facilities, experiencing pain or grief, or anyone who may benefit from a little prayer hug. By keeping the prayer shawls in the public context of worship, it can remind people of this ministry, should they wish to participate or support it; it also reminds people of the opportunity to request a shawl for a particular person they may wish to be gifted in such a way.

This type of practice can be done individually or as a group; some faith communities will have knitting circles, where people come together to share their prayers and praises while they enjoy being in each other's company as they create their wares. Some shawls are specifically created for individuals or circumstances, using a person's favorite colors, for example, or adapting a pattern for a shawl to fit a person in a wheelchair.

How Do I Do It?

Start with the premise that every stitch is a prayer. Keep in focus throughout the time of the benefit and purpose of the garment you are working on.

Set a time to be intentional about the practice. This is not a time to listen to a novel by audio or chat casually with friends; it is a time of prayer during which the creative act represents the holiness of the time.

If gathering with others, make sure everyone knows the purpose of the gathering and is of a similar intention to this ministry.

Choose a pattern and yarn for the project, suitable to the desire.

Begin with prayer. It may be as simple as a mantra from Scripture. Psalm 139:13 reminds us of our connection to God: "For it was you who formed my inward parts; you knit me together in my mother's womb."

Knit, crochet, weave. Offer prayers of intercession or thanksgiving; infuse the creation with love and holy intention. Let the Spirit guide your needles, hook, or loom.

When there are sufficient shawls to be blessed, request that the pastor/priest include the blessing within the worship; the time of offertory is a great way to uplift this ministry as an oblation of the church.

It may be a practice to include a note or card about the shawl or blanket, letting the recipient know that the piece was made with prayerful intentions and with love, reminding them of their value to the praying community in the church. Some cards may include a prayer for the recipient to pray.

Thank God that the minister or pastoral visitation team are distributing the shawls as an expression of God's love and the church's care.

FINE ARTS

What Is It?

The fine arts are an outlet of creativity, wherein the artist both receives the gift of doing the art and offers a gift of the art itself. (This does not mean that art needs to be given or even seen by anyone else, but the very act of creating art brings that to the world.) The art conveys a message, provoking an emotional reaction, possibly educating, or communicating a truth. In a very real way, art reflects the artist's view of, and experience of, the world.

Art is creating with intention, through contemplation and introspection to move towards a bigger picture of understanding the world and our place within it. Art can be created for ceremony (such as a religious commemoration or cultural piece) or functional purposes (beautifying the ordinary), as a means of persuading (such as motivational posters), as the artist's personal expression (a collage or abstract piece that is accompanied by interpretation), or as a shared narrative (such as a piece of history).

By participating in creation, we do not put ourselves above God, but immerse ourselves into the co-creating act. Art is often used as a means of therapeutic self-expression, allowing the artist to loosen inhibitions and limitations and engage with the imagination and free-ness of the interior. By being intentional about using this creative practice as prayer, it embraces the inner self and invites the Spirit to move in artistic ways. We invoke the power of God to make our artwork a tangible expression of our most inwardly prayers.

In this section, we consider several forms of fine arts which demonstrate a similar genre and, thus, comparable prayerful expression and experience.

- *Painting*: This uses paints to create a new image. While mostly two-dimensional, various techniques and methods are used to create a piece of art. These can include shading, brush strokes, perspectives and dimensions, or adding thicker layers of paint in expressions that are impressionist, abstract, realistic—anywhere the artist feels inspired.
- *Multi-Media*: Similar to painting, and often incorporating paint, this practice uses a variety of media to create the image. Most often, this begins in a two-dimensional format (such as painting on canvas or a photograph) and adds other aspects to add physical depth and contrast (e.g., forms made of clay, old keys, nuts and bolts, rocks, pieces of glass), which deepen the impact of the artwork.
- *Sculpting*: This practice involves the intentional construction or building up of the piece, creating a three-dimensional figure, such that the image is to be viewed from all angles (frequently using clay, but other substances are possible). This allows for different means of expression and interpretation for the artwork.
- *Carving*: Like sculpting in reverse, this format begins with a formless mass (e.g., wood, clay, marble, foam), from which the artist intentionally pares down layers until their piece is revealed. In removing these layers, a new form emerges; some artists understand this work as liberating the image from the external layers that had confined it within.

The media used for these forms of art can change drastically: painting may include acrylics on canvas or graffiti on a wall; multi-media may incorporate fabrics or cutlery; sculpting may display in marble or a decorated cake; carving may be in marble or a whittled piece of wood. The practice may be temporary or permanent, an original work or following a template; it may be contemporary or classic; it can be for public display or private appreciation. Whatever the creation is, the intent of creating is the purpose.

How Do I Do It?

Set aside time to be creative.

Set the scene! Determine which of the fine arts is speaking to you. Be open to trying new things.

Prepare your supplies. This may mean acquiring the basic media (paint, clay, soapstone, etc.) and the tools (canvas, brushes, plaster, etc.) yourself, or it may mean purchasing a pre-formed package (like a wood model kit or a paint-by-numbers set). It may mean signing up for a class where someone else will provide supplies and instruction (like a pottery class or paint night event).

Pray: invite God to journey with you, that the deepest desire of your heart may be known in your artistic adventures.

Create! Without the limitations from the world (or yourself). Embrace the art with reckless abandon, like a child enthusiastically finger painting or assembling a balsa wood model dinosaur. Don't worry if it is perfect or as intended, or even recognizable. The purpose of prayerful art is authentic prayer, not an effort to be spotlit in a gallery.

Be gentle with yourself. All practices take time; few are such strong visual reminders of our early stages in the efforts.

Consider our role as a creation, carefully loved into being: "O Lord, you are our Father; we are the clay, and you are our potter; we are all the work of your hand" (Isa 64:8).

Decide when you are done; there does not need be a set end time or stage in the creation. You can return to the piece as often as you like, to continue or undo or amend.

After each time with the art, thank God for the time of creating, for the freedom to make the art, and for the prayers that are encapsulated therein.

Clean up after your creative time. The process of cleaning can itself be prayerful!

COMPOSING MUSIC

What Is It?

Any creative exercise begins as a response. The urge to create, the ideas that spark the urge, the talents, abilities, and yearnings that enable these desires to bear fruit are all responses to the presence of God who has given them in the first place.

Writing or composing music can be a powerful expression of this deep connection between giver, gift, and recipient. The composing process draws on multiple layers of experience; words and/or notes come from deep places within and are woven together to express the prayers of our hearts.

Our compositions may be joyful and exuberant; they may be quiet and contemplative; they may be angry and pain-filled; and they may even, at times, seem dull and lifeless. Remember that the goal is not to impress others or even to play the composition *for* others. It is a prayer from your core that is created and offered to the One who created your core, who knows your core, who lives within your core, and who is inviting you to explore the vastness of the love that is at the core of God's very being.

How Do I Do It?

There are a multitude of ways to engage with musical composition as prayer. You could write your own words and melody, write a new melody for existing words, write new words for an existing melody, write music with no words—however you feel the music reflects your prayer.

Prepare yourself in a time and space where you have access to what you need—musical instruments, score paper, pencil and eraser (or pen if you're experienced!), recording devices, or whatever technological devices you require for the process.

Offer your time to God, recalling that the process is as important as any song which may result.

You may feel inspired to compose a piece with a specific theme: a season of the year (e.g., spring), a season of the church year (e.g., Lent), a specific personal experience (e.g., the death of a loved one), or a news headline (e.g., the discovery of a new planet).

You may not have a particular thought in mind. In this case, you might try to pick a topic at random, or select a musical style with which you are familiar: an anthem (a song for a choir during worship), a hymn for a congregation to sing, a psalm, a children's prayer, a lament, a rant.

There are even stories of songwriters who simply sat down at the piano, began playing random chords, and singing the first words that came to mind, and that turned into a song! This, too, is prayer.

Learn to trust the presence and leading of the Spirit in your writing, your composing, your singing, and even in your writer's block.

Whatever ends up being composed (no matter how refined or unpolished it may be), receive it as the gift it is. Offer it as the gift it is. Celebrate it as the gift it is. And if you feel called to share it, by all means, do so; your musical prayer may just be the prayer that someone else needs.

WRITING POETRY

What Is It?

Whether written down or spoken aloud, poetry uses words themselves as pieces of art. Words in poetry are used not just to communicate information; they engage us in a dialogue that expresses emotion, explores mysteries, proclaims truths, and invites us into the adventure of wondering.

This applies just as much when we are writing as when we are reading poetry. We are using the gift and art of language to express our deepest selves, to attempt to penetrate beyond the surface of existence and touch our meaning, to connect to the mystery of our being, our place in the cosmos, and our relationship with the one who has placed us here.

The deep connections between poetry and prayer are obvious and numerous!

How Do I Do It?

There are many ways for us to write poetry as prayer. You may choose a structured format, such as a certain number of syllables per line (as a haiku or a limerick), or find words that rhyme, which can end each line or stanza (hymn writers frequently use this device). Or, you may use a spoken word art form, which relies on emphasizing similar sounds in the words to provide anchor points for the listener instead of a set number of syllables.

Alternatively, you may use a free-verse form, simply putting words together (in a list, on a line, in a circle, etc.) without worrying about sentence structure, rhythm, or rhyme. Take a look online at some examples of so-called "refrigerator poetry."

Your poem does not have to be of a certain length or fill a required word count. As with anything creative, some days, the words will pour out of you, and some days, you may come up with three—or even none. Allow the process to be what it needs to be, always aiming for honesty, authenticity, and realism, because these are all important aspects of prayer.

Here is an example:

DUST BUNNIES

Written in 2024 by Rick Pryce

Sometimes
I'm not sure what to say
The words won't come
Amid the jumble of thoughts and feelings
Deadlines and hassles
And trying to name my stuff
Honestly
Just makes it harder (or impossible)

So
Here I am
Here's my mess
Here's my stuff
All on the cluttered floor of my life
Without order
Without category
And without hiding any of it

(Even the dust bunnies)

Help
Help me admit my stuff
Help me embrace my stuff
Help me even love my stuff
Not because I'm so needy
Or my stuff has so much potential
If only it was organized better

Or thought about differently

Help
Because of who you are
Who you have promised to be
Who you have shown yourself to be
Eternal lover
Persistent welcomer
Consistent embracer
Of the entire cluttered floor of my life

Even the dust bunnies

COLORING

What Is It?

The trend of adult coloring books came about some years ago, inviting adults to engage in a creative process. The act of coloring itself can be invigorating and help to reduce anxiety and stress, while increasing focus and meditative state.

The materials used are secondary to the process itself; you can use school crayons from a dollar store or expensive markers from an art supply store; you can color on blank paper or free print-out sheets or a formalized book. The images may be complex or simple, abstract or realistic. Some coloring sheets will be intentionally Christian; they may portray Scripture verses or themes in words.

The colors you choose do not need to be how the image appears in real life; this is a creative prayer process (not an art class). (For example, a camel can be shades of pink and green, a forest can be violet and red.)

How Do I Do It?

Quite simply, color.

Whatever the subject of the coloring, recognize the image it portrays as a gift from God.

However you feel inspired to color, do so! You do not need to color between the lines; you do not need to limit one color per space; you do not need to finish the piece; you do not need to follow any preconceived or conventional "rules" for coloring.

Be attentive to your coloring and what your style and choices might reflect. For example, is the choice of coloring image significant? What meaning do the colors that you choose have for you? Is your coloring hard or soft? Are you filling every space or leaving some blank?

Consider how God is speaking to you when you are in the act of coloring.

Meditate on what God may be communicating to you through your process and in the time. What thoughts have emerged? What has been revealed that can influence your spiritual life?

When you are done, you can do with your artwork whatever you please—recycle it, put it on the fridge, leave it in the book, etc.

Thank God for the time to color, and for the positive benefits you have received from it.

Reverse Coloring

A new take on this practice is reverse coloring, where a page is designed with colors in an abstract, watercolor format. Intended as a gentle guide to inspire creativity, the person then adds lines, shapes, or figures to the visual aid, allowing their creativity to establish shapes around the colors. Alternatively, the drawer can increase the abstract nature of the artwork, with dots, doodles, or lines, not to create a concise image but to allow the movement within the color to take on new meaning.

Just as the practice of coloring allows the person to add prayer to their creative practice, so, too, does reverse coloring. It follows a similar format, where we relinquish our artistic control to how we feel inspired to respond to the work before us. In recognizing this as a forum for reflection and prayer, we can move more deeply into the creative reality that God has included within us.

PHOTOGRAPHY

What Is It?

Simply put, it is using a camera to capture images of our world.

Looking at life through a lens changes how we look at life. We become aware of color, shapes, composition, and even movement. We start to look for different perspectives; we search for new ways of seeing, expressing, and capturing a vision, which no one else can see until we click the shutter.

And this applies even if all we have done with a camera is take photos of family during holiday seasons and birthday celebrations. We capture moments; we remember when we were together. Our relationships are acknowledged, affirmed, and deepened.

Looking at God's good creation with these new eyes, we can discover a freshness in everything around us, within ourselves, and even in our relationships with our Creator. As Jesus said to his friends as they were discovering new sight in his presence, "Then turning to the disciples, [Jesus] said to them privately, 'Blessed are the eyes that see what you see!'" (Luke 10:23).

Which is why photography can absolutely be a form of prayer.

How Do I Do It?

There is technical advice that will answer this question, but this is not a photography instruction manual! Fortunately, with the widespread availability of digital cameras (in our phones or as stand-alone devices), photography is incredibly easy.

Option One: A Walk

Take your camera (in whatever form you have it) for a walk around the block. Keep it short; stay in familiar territory. Let God speak to you in the ordinary.

Look for something you haven't seen before. Or look at something you *have* seen before.

Look at it through your camera. Don't even take a picture yet! Just look.

What do you see? What do you notice? What new thing is brought to your awareness?

Now, change the angle: try kneeling down on one knee, tip the camera 45 degrees, or take a couple of steps toward, or away from, your subject. Or even go across the street and look back at it. How has your vision changed?

Appreciate what God has shown you, just in this little exercise.

Now, go to whatever perspective spoke most to you, and take your photograph. Take several. What new vantage points come to mind? Take another picture. Or six.

Continue your walk. Repeat as you feel led.

Option Two: A Family Gathering

Take some spontaneous pictures of family members doing what they are doing. Talking, playing cards, swimming, whatever.

Gather a group (maybe some who wouldn't normally appear in a photo together (cousins, all the aunts, etc.). As you look through your camera, are you aware of new dynamics? Different possibilities?

Try kneeling down on one knee. Or change the angle from which you are taking your picture. How does that change what you see in your family? From what perspective is God seeing your family? How do you see God present within your family? Has it changed?

The Final Step: Editing

This is an important part of photography, and it has massive implications for our life with God.

First, not every picture will come out. The focus might be off, the subject may have moved, someone may have blinked, or you may simply find that the end result does not match what you thought you were seeing.

This is to be expected, and it is okay.

Second, you won't need seventeen versions of the same tree branch. Pick one or two that you like and delete the rest.

Third, remember that God does not expect perfection from us in *any* aspect of our lives. It's okay that not everything will come out. Enjoy the freedom that comes from not needing it all (our pictures, our relationships, our lives) to be flawless.

So, as you hit the "delete" button, give thanks! For your time of photography, for your time walking around the block or spending time with family and friends, for the new visions you discovered through your camera, and for God's abiding presence in all of it (even in the photos that don't turn out).

ARTISTIC SCRIPTURE

What Is It?

This form of prayer connects a passage of Scripture to a creative art format. It is not merely doing artistic things, it is being present to how God is speaking to you through the words of Scripture and your response. It is a deeper focus on a smaller portion of Scripture in a way that you engage the creative self with the words on the page.

This prayer invites you to step away from any inhibitions about being a creative creation of the Creator. Remember that what you produce is not meant to be subject to art critics nor necessarily of gallery quality. It's simply allowing yourself to engage in the creative process based on the word of God.

The process itself may be done individually or in a group; it can be a reaction and/or response to the word of God, a reaction and/or response to something that has happened in our world, or as a way to artistically augment a reading of Scripture. It may be concrete or abstract, using words or not. The art that you create is the prayerful way that your inner self is engaging at this time with the Scripture or circumstance being offered.

How Do I Do It?

Option One

Choose a passage (from the daily or weekly lectionary).

Read the Scripture aloud.

Identify what sentences seem to speak to you and print those out on a sheet of paper. It can be handwritten, or artistically written (such as calligraphy), or in a simple font through the printer.

Noting what word or phrase comes to mind as a first reaction, contemplate what image(s) now comes to mind. This can be abstract or concrete, silly or serious. It does not need to be explained to others.

Allow your innate creativity to draw what you are feeling: this may be doodling on the words of Scripture; it may be creating a reaction to the story in the passage; it may be an outpouring of the emotions the passage has evoked.

You may incorporate the words themselves, expressing them in different colors or fonts, creating word clouds, or color-coding the pieces that seem to connect for you. You may consider how manuscripts were in medieval times, with artistic flares to enhance and intrigue the reader (even if they did not directly correlate to the message of the passage).

Prayerfully consider how the art has enhanced your understanding of the word of God. Has new insight been offered? Did you previously connect colors or patterns with that piece? Does it remind you of other passages because of the artistic expression you've experienced?

Express gratitude to God for the opportunity to have new revelations on the Bible passage.

Option Two

Choose a passage (from the daily or weekly lectionary).

Read the Scripture aloud.

Pray silently about the passage and consider imagery that results. This imagery does not need to be confined by the norms of the world. For example, Phil 4:7 ("Do not worry about anything, but in everything by prayer and supplication with thanksgiving let your requests be made known to God") may inspire a concept of being held in prayer that is imagined as concentric circles of deepening colors; or a reflection on Ps 139:13 ("For it was you who formed my inward parts; you knit me together in my mother's womb") could show needles knitting cosmic yarn that has been spun from the stars.

Create that image on a sheet of paper, using whatever medium is easiest; pastels or watercolor may be best if the imagery you are considering is abstract, whereas more precise media, like markers or pencils, could be beneficial if you have a more concrete image to display.

Generally, this type of art will not include specific words written on the page.

Once the art is created, read the passage again and consider the piece you have made. Reflection may include if the image on the paper is comparable to what you had in your mind before you started? What does the image show that is unexpected? What were you expecting that isn't there?

A further piece of this is to take a bifold mirror and place it on your artwork at varying angles and locations. The resultant view, as only a portion of the art is refracted and multiplied, may reveal new considerations for your prayers. Why is this new image reflection important to you? How is God speaking to you through a multiplication of the existing art? How does the reflection process amend what is seen? Does this new meaning still relate to the word or phrase you were first drawn to?

Express gratitude to God for the opportunity to have new revelations on the Bible passage.

PRAYER FLAGS/CLOTHESLINE PRAYERS

What Is It?

With origins in Bon and Tibetan Buddhism,[1] prayer flags are colorful pieces of cloth that are strung together. Often found in the Himalayas, these flags repeat in five colors (blue for sky, white for wind, red for fire, green for water, yellow for earth). Tradition indicates that the balance of the elements establishes and maintains health and harmony. Each flag is woodblock-printed with a central symbol and particular prayers and mantras, indicating the traditional teachings and embracing the opportunity to pray. The presence of these flags also reminds passersby to pray for the person who hung them and for the well-being of the community.

Christians could respectfully borrow (not co-opt) a similar practice, to benefit from the essence and intention of our Buddhist siblings, by finding ways to create a form of bunting-like prayer cloths. This can be an especially practical prayer style at special events (like summer camp or Vacation Bible School), serving both as a decoration and as an invitation to pray. The colors could represent different aspects of prayer (such as thanksgivings, community prayer, prayer for the sick, etc.) and be hung up for all to see. Likewise, for communities of people for whom the written word is not easily accessible, a combination of colors and drawings could be a welcome form of expression.

These cloths can be as simple or as complex as desired; from drawing on rags with markers to paper printed with potato blocks, from embroidery in delicate fabric to stickers on premade plastic dollar store decor. They can be carefully put together by string or twine, or even hung individually on a

1. See "Interfaith Issues" in the introduction.

clothesline by pins. The intention is to share a prayer that is not dependent on any particular time, ability, language, etc.

How Do I Do It?

Select and collect your materials.

Create an intentional pattern, identifying a purpose for each color.

Create your prayers! Allow the Spirit to move your heart into areas you wish to share with anyone who sees. (They don't need to understand the intention of your prayers, as these are your prayers. But we never know whose hearts may be impacted by the prayerful encounters we have been a part of.)

Arrange your prayers so all colors are equally represented in order.

Hang your flags!

Your prayer flag system may be a growing entity (adding a new series of colors each day) or it may be completed in one sitting.

Let the flags become sun-bleached, rain-washed, weather-worn. They are being released to the world and to the source of love.

Chapter 7

Writing

JOURNALING

What Is It?

A Prayer Journal is not a diary, categorizing daily events, but an opportunity to focus on moments of insight and inspiration, which allows for breathing space in our daily walk with God. In a safe and private space, this journaling invites honest contemplation of the interweaving of Scripture, events, theological reflection, and insights to focus on the action and direction of God. It is intended to help us refocus aspects of our life in a meditative way so that we can look back on and discern trends and patterns in our lives.

Journals can be on a theme (gratitude, daily Scripture verse, dreams, etc.) or they can be less structured. They can be done daily, weekly, or whenever the Spirit moves; they can be written in whatever format is most comfortable (pen and paper, typed in a blog, doodles in color, etc.). The journaling format can incorporate other prayer practices of creating prayers (some of which are mentioned above).

How Do I Do It?

Start with a clean page. This can be in a dedicated journal or an individual sheet of paper, but each experience should be a fresh page that is not going to be mixed in with papers for other purposes (i.e., a diary or grocery list), nor as a direct continuation from a previous session.

Start each page with the day and the topic (whatever event, relationship, scriptural passage, or reflection has inspired you to journal).

Pause and pray. Ask God for help in clearing your mind of distractions; invite God to be part of the journaling process with you.

Reflect on the topic, writing or doodling, recognizing not all questions will have answers:

- From an analytical perspective: What happened? How have I reacted and responded? What did I think about? Do I need to do something? What's the next step?
- From engaging your senses: What do I see? What colors are prevalent? What am I hearing? What smells are there? Are there textures involved? What do I taste?
- From an emotional perspective: How do I feel? What memories is it evoking? What are my primary emotions? Where is this sitting in my body?
- From a spiritual perspective: How am I sensing God in this? How is this affecting my relationship with God and with the faith community? How much influence will this have on my spiritual life?
- From a self-awareness perspective: What does my head say about this? What does my heart say? What does my gut say?

Once you have explored these many perspectives, reread what is written and consider these questions: In what ways do I recognize God's presence in this? What are my desires? What is God calling me to do? Are there patterns I see in my life?

When you have completed the day's journaling, offer a prayer of gratitude for the journey with God.

Note: An alternative format for journaling can be to blog, or to vlog, providing a digital format for the regular recording of this spiritual practice.

WORD PLAY/MAGNETIC PRAYER-ETRY

What Is It?

A playful form of prayer, this is similar to Magnetic Poetry. Magnetic Poetry was a trend from the 1990s that continues to have popularity, whereby a collection of words was individually created as small fridge magnets. As such, they could be arranged and rearranged in a type of word play. Various expansion kits were created of different languages or a tightly focused theme (for example, a Canadian edition includes the words maple, moose, and hockey). Kits were commercially available by the original company, and a number of spin-off resources began to emerge into the public sphere.

The original creator of Magnetic Poetry was an aspiring songwriter who appreciated the flexibility to scatter his inspiration as a means to overcome writer's block.[1] This type of maneuverability appealed to budding poets everywhere as Magnetic Poetry began to pop up on fridges and could be used in families to leave notes, by students at parties, by grandmothers rediscovering their love of words that a busy life may have gotten in the way of—the possibilities are endless. Playing with word magnets became popular as they can be used for seconds or hours, alone or in groups, and the words can convey messaging that transcends the normal lines on a page of written language. (Imagine words about growth presented in the shape of a flower). This two-dimensional art allows increased opportunity for expression, as rhythm and rhyme are not essential.

With this understanding of Magnetic Poetry, and embracing the Greek roots of the word "poet" (*poiētēs*) meaning maker, prayers can be formed from our inner maker. The fun of language and space provides not only permission to create but the tangible resource to do so—in a fun environment in whatever time is available.

There is no need for special magnetic kits, but some can be found that have spiritual focus. There is the option as well to have blank magnets upon which new words can be added that are pertinent to the people making the poem or prayer. Another work-around to personalize a kit (in a temporary way) is to use small sticky notes. Colors and sizes can vary by preference. Again, the options are extensive; the intention is not to be perfect but to express in a playful word-play our communication with the divine.

1. Magnetic Poetry, "Our Story."

How Do I Do It?

Let the Spirit guide you, use the words that you see to create prayers. Don't worry if you change the words over and over, or if it feels awkward or clumsy; the words are impermanent but the intention of prayer remains.

Move the words you want to a particular order, space, shape, or configuration. Use whatever time you want to, while your coffee is brewing or as an evening with friends.

You can leave the prayer as it is, or move the words apart again. You can record the prayer onto paper or computer; you can share with an online Magnetic Poetry group; you can take a picture on your phone. Whatever feels right to you!

DEVOTIONS

What Is It?

Essentially, this form of creating prayer is an oblation (an offering or gift to God). It is choosing a topic and creating a devotional focus: How do we devote our time, talent, and treasure to God? Devotions use a set amount of time to engage in reading and reflecting on a theme or passage of Scripture. In keeping this practice concise, the goal is to engage in this type of prayer as a means to go deeper into conversation with the Creator.

While the time of a devotional is short, it can influence your thinking throughout the day and invite ongoing reflection of how God is active in your life. Devotionals can be a daily or weekly practice; it is usually done alone.

How Do I Do It?

There are many different options for guided devotionals; while some do not follow a particular theme, others are based on that particular focus. They can be seasonal (popular times include Lent and Advent), demographically based (for women, men, or youth), topical (devotions for new parents or for retired people); the list is endless.

For those beginning devotionals, it may be easiest to become comfortable with the practice by following a guided devotional; using a format that works best for your comfort level (booklet, blog, social media, whatever).

The format may suggest time parameters or encourage journaling; it may pose questions to answer or provide a reflection; there may be specific prayers or prayer prompts.

Some people will engage in devotional practices without a particular guide, selecting a passage of Scripture and making their focus match. This is similar to studying and/or praying Scripture, but with tighter parameters on the Scripture passage. There is also a slightly different outcome (devotionals engage the question of how we devote ourselves to God; praying over Scripture is to understand how God is speaking to us through those Scriptures).

FAMILY PRAYER WALL

What Is It?

While the title for this type of prayer indicates family, we recognize that this word can convey a wide scope of possibilities, from the people you live with to those you share DNA with, to those you worship with. However you find authentic connection and relationship, you can find yourself in a family. We invite you to apply this in whatever context is familial to you.

The space is created and maintained as an intentionally safe space offered for prayers to be shared with each other, to be collected over an established amount of time, and then prayed together. It can be an ongoing process, inviting collaboration in prayers surrounding meaningful issues to the family and its members.

How Do I Do It?

To begin, establish a space for the family's prayers to be posted and shared. This can be physical or digital, but it does involve communal access and engagement. It is similar to a bulletin board where folks can post their prayers: thanksgivings, petitions, intercessions, oblations. Ensure the method is comfortable for all members to use.

Next, make sure that everyone has access to the necessary resources and knows that they can add to the wall at any time. This could be done through a shared computer-based document, especially if the family is separated by distance or different times. In a physical space, the designated space could utilize a white board, a sticky wall or sticky notes, paper with tacks—whatever works for you.

The board could be thematic or without prescribed focus; you could propose a wall on a particular section of Scripture, or a theological motif, or reflecting on the news of the day.

At the end of week, month, or agreed time, gather as a family and pray the prayers aloud. This is a time without judgment or criticism and accepting of all the prayers that arise. It can be helpful to allow space for further discussion of the issues and prayers and embrace whatever new insights arise.

There may be ongoing discussion about the process and finding the best practice for the family. The prayer wall may be divided into sections, if this is useful.

WRITING FICTION

What Is It?

"There is no greater agony than bearing an untold story inside you."[2] This quote by Zora Neale Hurston encapsulates the recognition of something dwelling within us and seeking an outlet. Whether the story emerges as a novel, short story, or play, fiction can provide an outlet for a prayerful expression of the divine within.

In writing fiction, we are free to root our prayers in a setting of our choosing (that can influence the story), to introduce characters who will think and speak and act in ways that we would wish the best for them, and to create plotlines that share a narrative that we need to tell. At any time, the writing of fiction allows us to immerse ourselves (and the intended readers) into a world that we can imagine to be.

This means that we have the power and responsibility to control what happens within that fiction. A storyline may get stuck in heartbreak, or it may focus on the triumph of love and care. It may be limited to an expression of anger and despair, or it may highlight the power of reconciliation and hope. It may be a conduit of disconnect or a celebration of love and community. Normally, fiction will weave between many experiences and emotions; the ending (of the book) is up to us.

2. Hurston, *Dust Tracks*, 220–21.

Writing fiction is a means to share the good news of God. It depends on us, as the author, to determine how the story will flow, and what its underlying message will be. The fiction does not need to be explicitly Christian or even identify prayer in the characters' lives, in order to be a prayerful experience for the one writing.

How Do I Do It?

Open each writing session with prayer, identifying your intention to keep the time as an act of prayer.

Outline a rough idea of your characters, setting, and plot.

Determine how your fiction will be best presented: short story, novel, play, musical? The format will help define the outcome.

Further identify and expand on each of the characters, settings, and storylines to ensure you can go back to their defining characteristics as you progress with writing. This may help to keep things in line and logical, to reduce plot holes, and to maintain consistency in the story.

Write. Recognize the gifts of words as a gift from God. Be choosy in your choice of vocabulary.

Write as much or as little as you feel is meant for that time; you can always go back.

Reread each segment, considering if this is how you wish to leave it at this point.

Notice how you feel about your connection with what has been written: are these reflections of your life and journey? Are they aspirations for your life? Do they convey things you wish to avoid?

Know that you can go back to your writing at any time; fiction is seldom completed in one experience. This prayer format will take much time, thinking, and visioning.

Editing! Be gentle with yourself in the process. What was written does not have to be permanent.

Thank God for being with you in the writing and for accompanying and guiding you in your words. Offer your work as an oblation.

> "Let the words of my mouth and the meditation of my heart be acceptable to you, O Lord, my rock and my redeemer."
>
> PSALM 19:14

Chapter 8

Written Prayers

PRAYING THE LORD'S PRAYER

What Is It?

THE LORD'S PRAYER IS quite simply the prayer that Jesus taught his followers, which the church has been praying, both corporately and individually, for two thousand years. It is often the first prayer that people learn, and even those who identify as non-religious often know its words and cadence.

It's interesting to note that there are two different versions of this prayer in the Bible. In one (found in Matt 6), Jesus teaches his disciples to pray in a way that is life-giving, to free them from having to follow "the rules" about praying "correctly." In the other version (Luke 11), Jesus teaches it to them in response to a specific question from his followers: "Lord, teach us to pray." Both versions are similar, yet each is also distinct.

There are a variety of aspects that go into this difference. The authors of the two Gospel accounts have different purposes in telling their stories and want to engage different aspects of the stories they are writing. While one version might be more familiar to us, neither one is "more appropriate." They both speak to us; they both speak *for* us; they both speak *in* us as we speak with God.

Different traditions experience different versions of this prayer beyond a variety of translations. Thomas Cranmer, for example, in writing the Anglican *Book of Common Prayer*, included two versions (a longer and a shorter) in the Daily Office's morning prayer, as a means to meet the spiritual needs and experience of all folks in the realm. This intentionally brought together Christians of substantially different theological and denominational leanings.

This can be immensely freeing because it means we are not tied to using one version, one exclusive set of words. Individuals can be praying this prayer differently, yet be motivated by the same Spirit and the same prayer.

Yet, using this prayer is also a powerful reminder that we are praying *as part of the church*, the community of Jesus' followers. We are approaching God, and we are responding to God's approach to us *together*. There is no such thing as a solitary believer. We believe together, we serve together, we worship together, and, in the Lord's Prayer, we pray together as the timeless community of saints . . . even if we are not in the same room.

How we learn the Lord's Prayer varies based on our traditions, which means we have much to teach each other and much to learn from each other. For instance, the Anglican Catechism treats the prayer as a unified whole, while the Lutheran Small Catechism spends time with each petition separately.[1]

How Do I Do It?

Read the Lord's Prayer. Take your time, don't jump ahead with the familiar words.

Use different versions. A variance in words or word order can invite us into deeper reflection in ways we are not anticipating.

Memorize it (if you are able).

Memorize a different version from the one with which you are most familiar (if you are able).

Recite it. Saying the words aloud can offer us a new perspective.

Pray one petition a day, and keep repeating that petition all day long.

1. For a prayerful approach to these, we recommend Johnson and Johnson, *Praying the Catechism.*

PRAYING THE PSALMS

What Is It?

While the psalter is part of our Daily Office, it is a small component (even for those who pray the Office). Recognized as the "Prayer Book of the Bible," the collected psalms engage the reality of everyday life and grapple with the unavoidable human emotions that result from those realities.

From curses to praise, they remind us to hide nothing from God, to trust in God's presence regardless of our circumstances (sometimes even going so far as to demand God's presence!), and to always praise God.

The psalms can provide an outlet for those feelings that we often don't want to admit, even to ourselves. Some of these songs are laments, others seem to suggest incurring violence; still others are humans asking God to exact revenge on their behalf. It is important for us to realize that these are not inviting action but providing a venting space to rid ourselves of the anger and fear that can creep into us. The very reality of these emotions serves as a reflection of our most inward visceral thoughts; by saying them aloud, we are denying them further purchase into our being.

Likewise, the psalms elicit from us praise that reaches to the core of our being. The psalms of jubilation and celebration that cover daily events and high festivals remind us of the glory of God. They direct our hearts and minds to the beauty of creation, to the benefit of community, to the awesomeness of God's presence. In these psalms of praise, we are uplifted by the assurance that we are joining ourselves to all of God's faithful people, across the ages and all distances, as together, we pray with the same intention of joy and oblation to our Almighty God. Alleluia!

Many theologians have invited us into deeper conversation with the psalms, and part of this journey requires us to find ways for the psalms to continue to speak to us today. Context is important; these songs of praise and prayer were written to be normal prayers for normal people. This is part of the accessibility of the psalms; if we limit ourselves to the precise setting of the authors, we can overlook the intent of the authors.

It is also worth noting that the psalms are music; the word "psalm" translates as "instrumental music" and refers to the words that accompany it. As such, these are poetic and lyrical. They were designed to be sung, to aid in the memorization of the words, and make them more easily prayed and taught. Many of the psalms in Hebrew have rhythm and rhyme and use of clever repetition to hint at more depth than what our English translations allow. Psalm 23, for example, references both rod and staff—two words for the same tool—to highlight its use in protection and guidance. Psalm 119's twenty-two sections correlate to the characters of the Hebrew alphabet, and each of the eight lines in those sections begins with the same letter; and in each stanza, a synonym for the Torah is identified.

Praying the psalms can remind us to play with God, with the language of faith, even with our own emotions, knowing and trusting that God has seen, heard, and felt it all before and goes through it all with us.

How Do I Do It?

Find a translation of the psalms that you prefer (such as the *Inclusive Language Psalter*). Spend time reading the psalms as prayers, not in conjunction with other Scriptures, and not from an exegetical intention. Allow yourself to share your whole self with God, as the writers of the psalms did. You can choose a psalm based on a particular theme (i.e., Ps 100 for joyful praise or Ps 23 for comfort), or start from the beginning and progress through, or select at random.

Identify the feelings that the psalmist is expressing. Identify your own feelings in the reading of the psalm. Where are the connections? Differences? Is there comfort in this? Discomfort?

Talk with God about these feelings. Name them. Allow yourself to feel them and even embrace them. The psalms remind us that our feelings are also part of our relationship with our Creator and are a normal and natural component of our created being. God created these feelings for us; the psalms gift us with an opportunity to explore them in a timeless, prayerful way.

PRAYERS OF THE PEOPLE, OR THE INTERCESSIONS

What Is It?

In our common worship, liturgical traditions engage in a practice called the Prayers of the People, or the Intercessions. These prayers are intended to ensure that the congregation is maintaining emphasis on aspects of life that extend from the personal to the community to the world. It is a practice of expanding the heart as we aspire to move our attention outward from the challenges and experiences of our personal lives to the needs of the world.

Leading these prayers is an art and a skill; it is important to remember that they are not the prayers of the person praying performatively in front of the congregation; instead, the person leading these prayers is inviting the congregation into prayers of, for, and by all the people. As such, this practice of prayer involves a lead and a response; usually, at the end of the prayer, there will be a few moments of silence for the congregation to call to mind their own understanding, request, and focus for that aspect of prayer. The leader will then invite a shared response with words like, "Lord, in your mercy," and the congregational response of, "Hear our prayer."

Some provisos: these prayers are not intended to be partisan or promotional; they do not need to be explicit in detail. While they may be influenced by the Scriptures of the day, they are not to be a mini-sermon. They are a framework that guides the words of the heart into God's space of peace, justice, and equality.

These prayers will be both petitions (prayers for ourselves) and intercessions (prayers for others). If they are expressed as a bidding prayer, the words are directed to the congregation (i.e., "Let us pray for the church"); if they are offered as intercessory prayers, they are addressed to God directly (i.e., "Lord, we pray for the church"). In the tradition of most mainline denominations, they will cover six focus areas: the church, those in authority, the local community, the world, the sick and those in need, and those who have died. Additionally, prayers of thanksgiving are appropriate year-round; especially during challenging times (such as during local tragedies or disasters), a weekly petition of gratitude helped many congregations maintain hope-filled and positive hearts.

These categories can cover a wide spread of material for shared prayer, but need not encompass all areas every week. They can be timely and reflect issues of any size that the community wishes to hold up before God.

The church refers to the assembly of the faithful, gathered locally and globally and in all ages. *Those in authority* can include people in all levels of leadership, church authorities, and political parties (remembering that we can be political but are not to be partisan). Prayers for *the local community* can touch on the issues and affairs of the people and place, considering those who travel, local businesses, climate impacts, various ages and stages (such as school children or residents in care homes), or any significant events and happenings that are shared. In praying for *the world*, some intercessions will reflect those places in the headlines, the environment and ecosystems, a partner church or diocese/synod, areas of conflict, or moving beyond to the reality that our Earth is not the entirety of God's creation—the cosmos declare the glory of God! Prayers for *those who are sick* address those ailing in mind, body, and spirit; cognizant that we are seeking spiritual wholeness from our divine healer, even if physical miracles and cures elude us. For those *experiencing need* (who are not necessarily "needy"), we remember that needs can extend beyond financial or physical resources to include needs of emotional and spiritual factors. Praying for *those who have died* is an opportunity to commend the soul of the departed to the hands of God, to remember those who grieve and mourn as a result, and to acknowledge our own grief.

In an age and era where privacy matters are significantly important, and in a time when many liturgies are being shared online (and thus are accessible beyond the immediate congregation), it is exceedingly important to respect peoples' privacy. In the prayers for the sick, for example, no one should name names unless those folks have given their permission to have their identity (and often their ailment) shared publicly. We recognize a desire to name names before God—and we are welcome to do so!—but we are to be mindful of who else may be listening to our words; especially, those leading the prayers need to be discreet to ensure that prayer time does not provide fodder for gossip.

In all these prayers, we remember that God already knows our needs and our ignorance in asking: this practice invites us to better align our prayer focus to the will of God active in our lives.

How Do I Do It?

Depending on the practice of your denomination and congregation, there may exist certain frameworks and parameters around this practice of prayer. Speak to your clergyperson or worship leader about how to get involved in this ministry. There may be an established group or practice with resources or education and mentoring available.

Chapter 9

Reading

LECTIO DIVINA

What Is It?

LITERALLY "DIVINE READING," THIS practice engages in seeking the divine through sacred text. Through quiet repetitive reading and reflection, our relationship with God can develop and grow through the written word. While this practice is predominantly based in the Holy Scriptures, it can also be exercised on other writings—collections of prayers, sacred treatises or commentaries, poetry, even novels. God's presence is sought in expected and unexpected places, where we are anticipating finding the teachings of the holy.

For each text, a passage is chosen. This works best when it is a decent length to sit with for intentional reflection, but not so long as to prevent going deeply into the text. This might mean two to four verses of Scripture, a short poem, or a paragraph of prose.

The chosen text is read four times in an intentionally slow process that invites deep reflection on the word of God. The text can be read from the same translation or different versions, in different voices or by the same person, or listened to if they are prerecorded. This exercise can be done individually or with a group of trusted prayer partners.

The *lectio* is one way for us to continue our relationship with Scripture, to be open to God's revelation continuing in our hearts, and to inspire us to holy actions in our lives. We can be surprised as we consider passages that we have heard before but are experiencing in new ways based on how we have grown (emotionally and spiritually) and where our journey has already taken us.

How Do I Do It?

Sit comfortably in a quiet place.

Ask for God's presence and guidance to be known. Ask God for help to have a quiet mind and open heart.

Read (*Lectio*): Read or listen to the passage selected. The reading should be at a calm pace, giving you enough time to deeply listen to the words. Identify what words or ideas speak to you without needing to identify why they speak to you.

Reflect (*Meditatio*): Read the passage again, this time paying close attention to the areas of focus from the first reading. Without analyzing the passage, why are these areas important? What is God saying to you through them?

Respond (*Oratio*): Read the passage a third time, taking note of thoughts and prayers as God calls you to respond. How is God inviting you to ministry this day? It can be helpful to write these down so as not to forget.

Rest (*Contemplatio*): Read the passage again for a fourth and final time. Let the words wash over you. Rest in them; contemplate how God is using this time to speak to you. If you are called to write or journal your experience, now is the perfect time to do so. These contemplations can be discussed with your group or with your spiritual director at a later time.

Consider the exercise as a whole. How are you feeling? Are you feeling called to a particular course of action? Have you had insight into your life that you were not expecting?

End your time in prayer.

GOSPEL-BASED DISCIPLESHIP

What Is It?

This structured prayer is a gift to the church by the Indigenous Ministries of the Anglican Church of Canada. It is primarily used in group settings such as meetings, where the emphasis is on shared learning and prayer, with the gospel at both the literal and metaphorical center of all discussions. It engages the message of Scripture, and our response to that, as a foundation for the work we do in life and ministry.[1]

We also recommend learning some traditional practices that enhance this practice, such as the Talking Circle, a model that encourages dialogue, respect, shared creation of learning content, and social discourse while providing a sense of interconnectedness and community. This fosters a sense of safe space for sharing information, identity, and authentic interaction.

How Do I Do It?

Have three translations of one Gospel passage prepared for reading.

Gather together, sitting comfortably in a circle.

Open in prayer, inviting God to be present to all and to open everyone's hearts to what they need to hear this day.

Invite one person to read the passage. In turn, have each person identify (without explanation) what word or phrase stands out for them.

Hear the reading in a different translation of the same passage from a different reader. In turn, have each person articulate what Jesus/the Gospel is saying to them.

A third reader proclaims a third translation of the same Gospel passage. In turn, share what each perceives that Jesus/the Gospel is calling them to do.

It is important when this is undertaken in a group to let everyone have a turn to speak uninterrupted. This is a time for sharing, not for correcting, debating, or dialoguing. Each may thank one another for their sharing.

Close with prayers of thanksgiving for the word of God.

BIBLICAL STORYTELLING

What Is It?

Biblical storytelling is an act of memorizing scripture and presenting it orally—just as the early church shared their texts. In learning these texts

1. Anglican Council of Indigenous Peoples, *Disciple's Prayer Book*. We strongly encourage those interested to visit https://www.anglican.ca/im/introgbd/ to access *A Disciple's Prayer Book*.

by heart, they become incarnational and are then shared with nuance, movement, emphasis, etc., which helps the message come alive in ways that words on a page simply cannot.

There are many groups who participate in intentional storytelling, whose stories or experience is not connected with church or Scripture. They connect with their texts, be they fables or wisdom teachings or other narratives, usually from the past, and are able to bring them to life in meaningful and understandable ways. The benefits of storytelling include strengthening memory, improving verbal and aural skills, advancing creativity, imagination, and curiosity, and increasing cultural understanding and appreciation.

Learning biblical stories by heart is more than just memorization, for that is an academic exercise. Learning the stories for a shared telling is intended as an activity that allows for deeper understanding of the word of God and a stronger connection with the word through the words. The learning and remembering of the passage(s) lead to an internalizing of the story, which makes this itself an act of prayer.

Telling the stories is part of the process, and it is a culmination of many hours of prayerful practice. This may be done as a narrative proclamation of the word in a church service or as a member of a storytelling event (I once participated in the presentation of Mark's Gospel as a Holy Week offering!). The telling of the story is not a performance but a prayer—an act of praise, of oblation, of community, as the words float between those who speak and those who hear, connecting one another through the gifts of God.

How Do I Do It?

See how storytelling is done in person or through an online offering.

See how biblical storytelling is done. It may be attending a telling or a workshop. There are groups that can be helpful to do this (such as the Network of Biblical Storytellers).

If you will participate in an event, speak with the coordinator about your part. (Often, tellings have multiple tellers in succession.)

Pray over the available passages, seeing if any speak to your heart as meaningful.

When a passage has been selected, read it several times in its entirety.

Read it aloud. It may be helpful to record yourself to help you pay attention to what is heard.

Focus on the passage as though you are a participant or first-person witness. Consider the setting from your senses: what noises, aromas, and so on are present? Contemplate how you may have felt to have been involved in the event. Put yourself in many characters' perspectives as you read and reread the text, aware of the emotions of their interactions.

Meditate on the passage, asking for insight.

Describe it in your own words.

Study the words of the passage itself, making note of patterns, rhythms, references, etc. Mark down what is standing out to you, so you can go back and learn more from a historical or cultural perspective later on.

Start memorizing. You can read one line at a time, over and over, until you know it. Then add the second line, and do the same. Call to mind the emotions and sensory perceptions you identified in the first few readings.

As you engage in memorization, be active: you can walk, sing, do laundry, cook, etc. When you engage your body as you recite the lines, it becomes easier to feel them as natural and as a part of you.

You may wish to draw out a storyboard, or to make particular notations in a graphic way, to guide you in the learning of the story. Words are to be avoided; extra words can complicate the process rather than simplify it.

Keep practicing; internalizing anything can take time; doing so with spiritual words carries with it the potential for longer timelines.

Invite others to hear you! Tell the scriptural story to people you trust, who can then offer you support and constructive feedback.

Be gentle with yourself; this is not about perfect memorization but about prayerful and faithful recounting. A high goal is to have 80 percent of the words accurate in the retelling.

PRAYER STATIONS

What Is It?

Traditionally, the stations of the cross is a series of fourteen stations that depict significant events in the last day of Jesus' life on earth: Jesus is condemned to death; Jesus carries his cross; Jesus falls the first time; Jesus meets his mother; Simon of Cyrene is made to carry the cross; Veronica wipes Jesus' face; Jesus falls the second time; the women of Jerusalem weep over Jesus; Jesus falls the third time; Jesus is stripped of his garments; Jesus is nailed to the cross; Jesus dies; Jesus is taken down from the cross; Jesus is placed in the tomb.

Each station is represented by an image and invites prayer and reflection as the individual or group journeys through the stations. At each station, there is some variation of a prayer ("We adore you, O Christ, and we bless you. Because by your holy cross you have redeemed the world") and a relevant passage of Scripture. Some services will be led by someone carrying a cross, and a suitable hymn is frequently sung as people walk between the stations.

This becomes a mini pilgrimage for those who are otherwise unable to engage in a pilgrimage to the Holy Land. Some places offer permanent stations either inside or outside (depending on their facilities) so that they can be prayed at any time; often, churches will also engage in this practice as a scheduled time for community prayer during Holy Week or as part of the triduum.

Following this pattern, this prayer incorporates art, movement, and written prayer; in some cases, there is also music.

There are a number of possible formats for stations that have emerged from this type of practice. These can include (but are not limited to) the following.

- Traditional Stations: As described above, these prayers guide the faithful through the Good Friday event with reflection and prayer. It is important to note this is not a reenactment but a spiritual journey. It can also be helpful to note that not all of the fourteen stations have a direct scriptural reference but are rooted in long-standing devotional tradition and teaching (such as Veronica wiping Jesus' face).
- Biblical Stations: These stations intentionally focus only on those narratives that can be found within the passion narratives in the Gospels.
- Other Biblical Stations: These will focus on a particular event, selecting other significant biblical stories to engage with in prayerful depth. Some examples of this can include the Epiphany story from Matthew's Gospel (see appendix 1 for one such example), the coming of the Holy Spirit at Pentecost in Acts, or the theme of holy pilgrimage throughout history. The *Via Lucis* (or *Way of Light*) is a pattern of fourteen stations that encourage the journey beginning with the Resurrection through Pentecost.

- New stations can be created that are seasonally based for the church year. These engage other biblical teachings as a companion in the liturgical calendar. Many churches offer an Advent or Christmas service of "Nine Lessons and Carols," which connect Scripture, prayer, and song in a way that guides an intentional journey.
- Stations can be topical or thematic, based on the world and our current concerns; for example, we have participated in stations on ecological suffering and stewardship, connecting to scriptural passages of creation. One might write stations of creation based on the first creation narrative in Gen 1, implementing two stations for each day ("and there was evening, and there was morning"). (See appendix 2 for one such example.)
- Another form of stations may be locally based, found in times of peaceful protest or community healing. These stations may journey through issues of injustice, seeking to engage with the topic in educational and biblical ways. Other settings may be as a community coming together to walk and pray through a shared space that has experienced violence or other devastation. The "Take Back the Night" effort is one such example. In such a prayer practice, locations for the stations need to be chosen with care (depending on circumstances, legal considerations might need to be kept in mind).

How Do I Do It?

When first learning the practice, it can be helpful to participate in a planned event being led by a local community. Alternatively, if one is not readily available, connecting with a church or community that has the visual focus or artwork permanently prepared can be helpful, as those communities tend to have people keen to share about the experience.

At the same time, it is not uncommon to see people using the stations as a personal devotion, making the journey through the story (and around the sanctuary or garden) on their own. Once one is familiar with the pattern and the flow of this prayer style, it can become a meaningful experience of, and response to, the presence of God.

It is helpful to remember that the stations may be an emotional time, addressing themes of abandonment, suffering, and death. The artwork may be evocative, the physical pathway may have minor obstacles (intentional or otherwise). While stations ultimately prepare us to dwell into the promise of hope that the risen Christ assures, it can be helpful to make these journeys with a trusted companion or spiritual guide. Sharing the journey with others can help add to the solemnity of the occasion, even if there is no further discussion of the event.

There are many resources that can be found online about the stations; we encourage you to embrace a local expression.

Chapter 10

Sacraments/Sacramentals

SACRAMENTS

What Is It?

DERIVING FROM THE LATIN for something that is holy or consecrated, a sacrament is often defined as an outward and tangible symbol of an inward and invisible grace. Here, we want to focus on the dynamics of the community in prayer, which we see as central to the practice of the sacraments.

While there are variances in theology about the number and significance of the sacraments, and we strongly encourage you to speak with leaders in your tradition to learn more about your experience, for the purposes of this chapter, we will address the two/seven typically recognized by most mainline Christian traditions.

Baptism (a rite of spiritual cleansing and initiation into the Christian community) and the Eucharist (or Holy Communion, the act of thankful remembrance of the Lord's Supper to acknowledge the covenant of Christ and our shared participation in the church) are two sacraments that are, at times, considered ordinances by Protestant or Anabaptist traditions. They are the two Christian rituals initiated by Christ, according to Scripture, and at these occasions, Jesus himself articulated and modeled the importance of communal prayer.[1]

1. Baptism in community: Matt 28:18–20; Acts 2:37–42, 10:44–48, 16:31–34, 18:8, 19:1–7. Communion in community: Matt 26:26–29; Mark 14:22–25; Luke 22:14–22,

There are five other rituals that were influenced by the Jewish traditions, which was the context of the apostles, and initiated by the early church. These are recognized as sacraments within much of the church. These include confirmation (or chrismation, a ceremony whereby the individual confirms the faith proclaimed at their baptism), confession (or penance, whereby sins are confessed and reconciliation with God is conferred by the clergy), marriage (a blessed union between two people), unction (or sacrament of the sick, whereby an ill or injured person receives laying on of hands and/or anointing with holy oil, with the intention of the cure of souls); and holy orders (ordination to particular ministries within the church). These rites are considered instituted by the apostles as they engaged in their ministry and can be found in the epistles of the New Testament and the history of the church. Again, prayers are identified as essential and particular to these sacraments.

In baptism and Eucharist, there are particular elements necessary for the sacrament to be performed (water for baptism, bread and wine for Eucharist), whereas the other sacraments depend on prayer alone. There are additional elements possible (but not required) in each of the rituals (such as candles or oil), but the distinction is worth noting.

The nature of sacraments are community-based and celebrate being part of our communal spiritual journey.

How Do I Do Them?

Option One: Participating Through Attendance

Due to the communal nature of sacramental prayer, it is not difficult to attend or participate in many of them. Showing up or accepting an invitation works for many.

The Eucharist is often celebrated weekly in many churches, where all those seeking the sacrament are invited to receive. (Many offer an option to receive a blessing from the officiating clergy, if the elements of bread and/or wine are not desired.)

Special services of baptism and confirmation are often celebrated within the context of a regular worship service, so those attending worship on those days will be a participant by nature of their presence. Invitations

24:28–32; Acts 2:42; 1 Cor 10:16–17, 11:33.

are not uncommon for these events for family members or friends, who make up the extended community.

Special events like marriages or ordinations tend to be set at a unique time, and people are invited to attend. These do technically remain public events and, as such, are open to all who wish to attend; though it is good manners to respect the wishes of the individuals at the celebration. The public nature of the sacrament does not extend to any receptions or after-parties.

For these sacraments, some form of discussion or preparation is advised. Often, churches will host classes to ensure that the intended participant understands the importance of what they are about to undertake. You can speak to your clergy for more information about the specifics within your tradition and your local community.

Option Two: Participating by Request

The sacraments of reconciliation and unction tend to be more private, due to the nature of the sacrament and the practicalities of space and circumstance. (One would not want to wander into the hospital room of a stranger to see what unction was about!) For these sacraments, a discussion with the clergy will provide guidance and direction.

Some traditions also celebrate Holy Communion in special situations (the home of a shut-in, the hospital room of the sick or injured, a prison cell of the incarcerated). These are holy moments and are reminders of the prayers of the wider community as well as the presence of God in every moment. Speak to a pastor, priest, or chaplain (if one is available) about your desire for Communion.

SACRAMENTALS

What Is It?

Adjacent to sacraments are items called sacramentals. As a noun (not adjective), these are unique items that are a physical entity that embodies an experience. They remind us of the sacrament itself long after the earthly time frame of the sacrament's ceremony. These items then extend the prayers, the intentions, the purpose of the sacraments in less formalized, less structured ways. Often, the item itself has been blessed within the context of the expression of a sacrament.

For example, someone receiving the sacrament of baptism is often given a candle, lighted from the church's paschal candle during the service ("Receive the light of Christ, to show that you have passed from darkness into light"). This, then, can serve as a reminder of the day, inspiring prayer and consideration of the gift received. The anointing with holy oil leaves a gentle oil upon the forehead in the sign of the cross, which can remind the recipient of the blessing given to them at baptism and confirmation.

Additionally, items can be blessed by clergy with the intention of serving as a means to engage in prayerful activity. This differs slightly from a reminder or symbol of prayer (see chapter 12), as they carry a different appreciation and understanding, having received a formal blessing for a specific prayerful purpose. A classic example is the rosary or prayer beads, blessed to be used by the faithful, to carry the blessing, and inspire the user to live, share, and extend the blessing. These items then create a new connection between the individual, God, and the church community, where the blessing has been offered. Some blessed items, as sacramentals, become heirlooms, treasured from generation to generation; jewelry or Bibles, for example, carry the tradition of intentional prayer.

These items are intended to be accessible by anyone at any time. Sacramentals are understood to be significant by the nature of the one using it. That is not to say that individuals can control God through their prayers with a blessed item nor a particular ritual (such as lighting the baptismal candle on an anniversary). Prayers offered while holding a blessed prayer book are not more powerful than the same prayers from an unblessed copy. Sacramentals serve to increase and strengthen the desire to pray, the commitment to living the Christian life, and the experience of being fully human.

How Do I Do It?

Respect the item that is a sacramental for you. This may mean keeping it in a safe space or dedicating a set recurrent time to pray with that item. You may wish to let loved ones know the significance of this item to you.

As part of your prayer, you may wish to be in contact with the item: wrap the prayer shawl around you, hold the blessed jewelry in hand, etc.

As part of your prayer, you may wish to have the item as a focal point: light the candle, have the Bible open to the passages you wish to read, etc.

If your item is connected to a particular set of prayers, you may pray those.

Remember the importance of that item and how it is for you an aide-mémoire of the physical presence of God active in your life.

Thank God for the community that supports you in your faith journey.

Thank God for the item that serves as a holy reminder and for the time spent together.

Chapter 11

Communal Prayer Time (Accountability)

"When two or three are gathered together in my name" (Matt 18:20).

We are called to pray together. We are blessed to gather in the name of the Holy One and raise up our prayers of thanksgiving, petition, intercession, and beyond. This is a sacred responsibility, however, and it is humbling to always bear in mind that the information we have been given, when we gather in prayer, has been shared in trust and is to be held in trust. The time of communal prayer is not a time to share gossip or pass along juicy tidbits; it is a time when knowledge is definitely *not* power.

PRAYER PARTNERS

What Is It?

This is an intentional relationship with a spiritual sojourner to empower and encourage prayer. They are not an expert, and this is not a professional relationship; this person is someone with whom you have decided to intentionally connect and pray.

Prayer partners will establish a prayerful support system of nonjudgmental accountability to the practice of prayer. This is a reciprocal relationship with benefits including strengthening faith, deepening relationship, offering support, and sharing in celebration. Over time, the prayer partner can help to identify patterns, bolster confidence, empower discernment, and offer fresh perspective. They can help us see things in new ways, to overcome weak spots, to articulate gratitude, and to walk alongside us, whatever is going on in life.

How Do I Do It?

Connect with someone who shares similar core values and spiritual beliefs.

Establish a pattern of communication and commitment. Regularly revisit the partnership. Articulating expectations to one another can help prevent miscommunications and disappointment (for example, maintaining confidentiality at all times).

Pray for your partner daily.

Regularly meet and pray together. Acknowledge that there will be times that flexibility and rescheduling will need to happen.

Keep the focus of prayer on your lives as you pray for each other; what is in your heart and in your experiences. This is not a prayer group (as they have a broader focus).

You may wish to identify a passage of Scripture that has been coming to mind in your prayers; your partner may have insight as to how that connects you with God.

Open your heart to a spirit of trust, and as your relationship deepens, allow yourself to be more vulnerable with your prayer partner.

Rejoice in the movement of the Spirit: praying with someone really can help us to see abundant and ever-increasing blessings in our lives.

PRAYER GROUPS

What Is It?

Very basically, this is a group of people who gather to pray. This is usually a group of people within a faith community who are committing themselves to hold up before God the people and situations that are important within that community.

It is incredibly important that the prayer group has clear parameters and expectations, such as sharing personal information, confidentiality beyond the group, and anonymity of some folks requesting prayers. Plainly put, what happens in prayer group stays in prayer group!

How Do I Do It?

If a prayer group already exists, then ask leadership to join! Each group will function slightly differently, based on their context of ministry.

If a group does not yet exist: identify a number of folks who feel called to pray. Invite them to join the group.

Identify leadership of the group. For example, who will compile the prayer list? Who will communicate with church leadership (to allow pastoral response)? Who will update the team of changes between meetings of the prayer group? Who will engage in difficult conversations if prayer time is feeling gossipy or if confidentiality is broken? (Those can be challenging conversations, often best dealt with by trained pastoral staff).

Articulate categories for prayers, such as major global events (wars or crop failure), those in authority (locally, nationally, globally), parish staff and volunteers, parishioners who are in long-term care facilities or otherwise limited mobility/independence, those who have requested prayers (privately and to be shared for the weekly intercessions in corporate worship), and those who have requested prayer but do not want their circumstances shared broadly.

Gather monthly.

Open and close every meeting in prayer. Someone may wish to offer a brief devotional or reflection within the allotted meeting time.

Together, go over the prayer list to ensure updated information. This also serves to prevent people from falling through communication gaps. If information about the person has been provided, it can be included in the confidential section; it can also help to identify who has asked prayers for those people. Remember, prayer requests are not limited to members of the parish; we all have friends and family who may experience challenges or thanksgivings and request prayer. Church prayer groups are privileged to be invited to pray beyond our walls/parish membership.

The prayer group prays the list in its entirety when they gather (usually, once per month). Identify particular prayer requests (such as "we pray for Susan who is experiencing barriers to graduation; we ask for wisdom as they navigate confusing systems").

The members of the prayer group also commit to pray the list daily (or as often as they are able). Updates can be shared at any time with the designated person who makes updates, who can share those updates with the group (possibly via confidential email) between meetings.

At all times, be sure to respect the privacy of those being prayed for. If someone wishes public prayers, a good practice is to use only their first name in the worship service (and not detail their ailments or other aspects of their prayer request!).

It may be that there are two levels of prayer group: the first being those who access the full list and pray daily, and those who access only the names on the public prayer list to pray daily.

Some prayer groups will also engage in prayer teaching or study, hosting workshops in the community, or reading through a book together.

PRAYER CHAIN

What Is It?

Not unlike a phone tree, this is a particular structure designed to share information in a speedy and expedient manner. These happen in times when prayer requests are urgent.

These are less common now that we live in a time of social media and email blasts, but they can still be quite helpful when time is of the essence.

It can be helpful to use social media to help share urgent prayer requests, providing it is a request appropriate to be seen beyond the parish (as social media is global). It may not be appropriate if the prayer request is not something to be written down.

How Do I Do It?

A chain or tree structure is created prior to there being an urgent need, like a phone tree where each person contacts three people; this allows the sharing of information to grow quickly without being burdensome to anyone.

Identify what clear, concise, appropriate prayer requests will be communicated.

One (authorized) person begins sharing the prayer request, thus starting the tree/chain. This can be by phone call, by text message, or other electronic means.

Usually, a prayer chain will be of a significant event that can be quite distressing (a car crash, for example); and it is important to remember that not all information about that event may be accessible; it's better to say "I don't know" than try to fill in the blanks.

PASTORAL SUPPORT

What Is It?

Much of pastoral ministry involves knowing when to be present and when to leave. Especially in cases of visits to hospitals or care homes, it is imperative to remember who it is that's in the bed: they get to decide how long a visit and prayer should be, regardless of the intentions and good heart of the visitor.

Pastoral support is, at its core, a spiritual companion in a time of distress or celebration. When a need is expressed, the pastor responds in an appropriate way, offering prayers and whatever else the individual or family may desire.

It is helpful/essential to remember what pastoral support is not: it is not counseling; it is not intervention; it is not a fix-all or magic cure; it is not an information gathering session; it is not medical advice. Generally, the person extending pastoral care is not trained for those aspects; they are, however, trained in prayer (and, ideally, in pastoral visiting).

It is a time to connect with another individual and with God.

Support is to be directed from the visitor to the recipient; it is not a mutual gathering for cyclical care. As relationships deepen, it can become mutually beneficial (and is not to be discouraged!). However, the purpose of the visit is to be clearly understood as a pastoral visit.

How Do I Do It?

When a pastoral visit is requested, the one offering pastoral support should arrange a time and space that is comfortable for the person being visited.

If your community is set up with things like prayer shawls or prayer cards, they can be brought along in the visit.

Show up!

Observe the basics of respect: ask if it is a good time to be there, if the person being visited still wants the visit (they may be feeling drowsy or uncomfortable; the life of a patient can change quickly and unexpectedly). Don't put anything on the person's bed (including sitting on the edge), as movements can cause discomfort and physical closeness may not be wanted. If others are visiting, you can offer to include them or to come back another time.

Recognize that a person being visited has allowed themselves to be vulnerable. This is a position of trust.

Let the person being visited guide the conversation. Do not ask them to share anything more than they are comfortable with.

Ask them what prayer focus they would like.

If your tradition does communion or anointing, you may ask if they would like to receive this. Respect their choice. Ask permission before touching the person, even on the hand or forehead.

Pay attention to the person; they have gone through something substantial (folks undergoing medical treatment need more sleep than normal, new parents may have needs they don't want seen, etc.)

Pray! As they wish, offer prayers to God for their condition. Offer prayers for their caregivers, their supporters, and all who are carrying them in their hearts.

Keep the visit brief; ask the person if they would like future visits.

Get permission from the person before sharing their location, condition, or personal information with anyone.

When you have left, thank God for the privilege of being invited into the trust of the person you've visited.

Chapter 12

Ordinary Moments

MEAL PRAYERS

What Is It?

ANYONE WHO WENT TO summer camp likely knows some gratitude songs that were sung before a meal . . . sometimes with a bit more energy than our camp counselors may have wished! (How many rousing renditions of "Johnny Appleseed" can you recall?)

The concept of offering thanks before a meal has a long tradition; long before we could simply stock up on groceries from the market, our ancestors depended on a successful season and abundant harvest to ensure adequate nutrition. As God has created all things, including the soil to grow our plants and pasture for our livestock, we extend gratitude for the gifts. In our modern times, we acknowledge those whose hands have been involved in the preparation of our meals, from the farmers to packers to transporters. Food scientists, whose research improves nutritional content, and safety inspectors, who ensure our well-being—there are many whose life's work ends up on our plates.

The practice of expressing gratitude for the meal has biblical roots, interconnecting the theology of gratitude and the agrarian reality. From the provision of manna and quail in the exodus, the people of God learned to share what they had, that all may live. Leviticus 23:22 starts the tradition of leaving the edges of crop fields unpicked, to provide sustenance for travelers and those in need. Many passages remind us of the opportunity to make use of our abundance to feed the hungry (such as Isa 58:7, Matt 25:35, Jas 2:15).

While some food offered to God was sanctified through specific prayers, all food is recognized as a blessing. The Eucharist demonstrates the practice of saying thanks before sharing a meal; a table grace extends a comparable invitation to recognize God's gifts in our midst.

How Do I Do It?

There are abundant resources for expressions of gratitude. A simple internet search can present hundreds of prayers of varying length and intention. Some examples attributed to our traditions include, "Come, Lord Jesus, be our guest, and let thy/these gifts to us be blessed. Amen." And "For what we are about to receive, may the Lord make us truly thankful. Amen."

Some families will hold hands; others may fold their hands. Some graces are sung; others are spoken. Some will circle the table and invite each member to articulate something they are thankful for that day. Some traditions suggest a different focus each day (our families, our colleagues and jobs, our friends, etc.)

Be patient with yourself, as it can take some time to become comfortable with this practice. But by establishing a practice of intentional gratitude, it connects us more deeply with what nourishes us, physically and spiritually. As medieval theological Meister Eckhart famously wrote, "If [one] had no more to do with God than to be thankful, that would be enough."[1]

REMINDERS/SYMBOLS

What Is It?

A mentor of mine had a bell tied to the rearview mirror in his car. When I asked him about its purpose, he shared that it had been inspired by a rabbi friend who said, "Every time the bell rings, I remember to praise my God." Thus, driving became an activity with a spiritual component.

Such mementos and symbols allow us to surround ourselves with reminders of the opportunity to pray and praise. They do not need to be

1. Eckhart, "Sermon 27" in *Complete Mystical Works*, 172–74.

explicitly Christian or prayer-focused (but they can be!); they do not have to have immediate roots in a spiritual or religious event (but they may!). The beauty of reminders is that they are unique and particular to us—they remind us to pray and praise. They do not need to remind our neighbor of our invitation to pray, nor are they for us to remind others that we feel they ought to pray.

Martin Thornton refers to daily colloquy as the small, unplanned prayers in those ordinary moments—from a prayer of gratitude for that first cup of coffee to a bedtime appreciation for a soft and safe place of rest, our days host abundant ways for us to enter into praise.

How Do I Do It?

The key is intentionality. Determine what holds meaning for you: an object or a symbol (like cross jewelry, a Bible on the bedside table, a bell in the car). The symbol(s) you choose should not just remind you of prayer but inspire within you the action. (Some of our visual prayer prompts include a paperweight, a coffee cup, T-shirts of church camp days with a community of prayer.)

Place these symbols around your living space in ways that they will be seen and useful.

When you see these reminders, pray.

BLESSING PRAYERS (INSPIRED BY THE *BERAKHAH*)

What Is It?

Rooted in Judaism,[2] this prayer is a format or style of thanksgiving, most often offered before food or praise for a commandment being undertaken. It can be done privately or publicly and is almost always a spoken blessing or benediction. This is rooted in Deut 32:3: "When I proclaim the name of the Lord, ascribe greatness to our God!"

A *berakhah* typically starts with the words "Blessed are you, Lord, our God" and addresses the particular blessing that is intended. In doing this, the praying person or community is celebrating God as the source of all blessings and acknowledging that blessings are abundant. There are three main categories of these blessings: before enjoyment (such as the

2. See "Interfaith Issues."

appreciation of food or fragrance), before beginning a commandment (such as lighting Sabbath candles or at a bar/bat mitzvah), and in praise or in gratitude for God's justice (such as hearing good news or of being overwhelmed in nature's beauty).

This expression of prayer is an invitation to not take things for granted but to express gratitude and praise in daily life.

It is important to recognize that the *berakhah* is a Jewish prayer practice, and it is just as important to be intentional about not trying to make it Christian. There is too much history of the Christian church claiming it has superseded the Jewish tradition; we do not want to encourage this manner of thinking or behaving in any way.

That being said, we believe we can appreciate the essence of the prayer practice as an intentional time of benediction in the moments of our lives.

How Do I Do It?

Ideally, speak with a practitioner of the Jewish tradition; a rabbi or synagogue leader may be able to help you to learn and understand more about this practice of prayer.

Learning from the example of the *berakhah*, engage in a practice of praise and blessing.

Be intentional about noticing moments of blessing in your life.

Articulate those through praise or benediction. Name the blessing and articulate why/how it has blessed you today.

Share them with others in your life, not in a forceful way but as an invitation to celebrate God's goodness.

When you hear others offering praise and blessing, respond with "Amen" in a respectful manner.

BED PRAYERS

What Is It?

Very plainly speaking, these are prayers at bedtime. This brief night prayer, at times called "compline" (from the Latin root for "completion"), was designed to be offered by families in the home immediately before bed. This time of prayer is intended to bring spiritual peace and a focus on the gratitudes of the day, leading into a time of silence.

Many traditions engage in some form of prayer before retiring for the night. These are different from an evening prayer (which offers a distinction between the working hours and the rest of the evening).

A time of quietness and reflection at the end of the day, the practice can be seen as part of a larger prayer service (such as part of the Ignatian examen) or, if in a group residential setting, as a clear marker of the end of the day. (Monastic communities begin the "Great Silence" after compline, a time of quiet where interaction is strongly discouraged until the morning light.)

Some groups (youth groups, secular groups, etc.) use exercises such as "thorns and roses," where each person identifies a challenge and a highlight from the day.

This basic focus of reflection is a release from the stresses of the day, bringing spiritual comfort and closeness with God. It also encourages a perspective of gratitude for the day that has passed, a request for protection through the night, and can address how one wishes to act in the next day.

How Do I Do It?

Chances are, at some point, we have all done this. From a child's "Now I Lay Me Down to Sleep," to kneeling bedside to list the people we wish God to look after, to counting sheep as symbols of gratitude, the desire is to bring order to the disarray of our lives.

One option is to simply list the day's joys and grace-filled moments, offering thanks to God.

One is to follow a prescribed written service, such as can be found in most mainline traditions.

A component of this time of prayer is to acknowledge the situations of the day that you wish had gone better and to let it be, as nothing can be changed at that moment. This is not to avoid responsibility but to allow a peaceful night to better address (and redress) any issues the next day.

Breathing deeply, with lights dimmed, allow yourself to relax into a peaceful repose.

WHEN SLEEP WON'T COME

What Is It?

We've all had nights when the brain simply *refuses* to "relax into a peaceful repose" (as we just said above). This difficulty might be stress-related; we have a big presentation in the morning, or we find ourselves on the horns of some kind of dilemma. We may have drunk too much coffee (or some such) too late in the evening. Perhaps, we watched or read the news, and one of the stories won't stop whirling around in our heads. Maybe you, like so many of us, have mental health issues, which can mess up your sleep patterns. Or you might be taking a new medication (some of these can act as a stimulant, making sleep a challenge).

Or maybe you just can't fall asleep! It happens.

We are not suggesting *at all* that praying during these times will solve the problem for you, or make everything clear, or enable you to let go and immediately rest. Prayer is not a panacea, a cure-all for whatever ails you.

What we *are* suggesting is that prayer is part of our relationship with the holy. It is a concrete way of responding to the gifts of life and faith, which give us our identity as God's beloved. Therefore, it is a way of reminding our over-worked and/or over-tired brain, that our inability to fall asleep on this particular night is not a sign of God's displeasure, or evidence of a lack of faith or value. No matter what is causing your sleeplessness, you are loved.

How Do I Do It?

The first step is to admit to yourself that you are having "one of those nights." Believe it or not, simply naming the reality in which you find yourself can be a huge relief. It identifies it as a thing that is happening; but it's a thing that does not define you as a person.

Naming that night's situation is a form of prayer. It acknowledges what's going on and gets it out on the table, so you can talk or think about it with the one who is with you in your sleepless night.

What comes after this acknowledgment is a more personal decision, which will be dictated by your own personality, needs, or perhaps, the cause of your restlessness. Some people find that, once they have named the problem, they can begin letting go right away and soon are sleeping. A simple "Thank you" will be a wonderful way to pray in that moment.

Others of us, depending on the situation, may need to get out of bed for a while. It is generally acknowledged that going to the computer or TV is probably not the most helpful thing to do right then. It can act as a distraction from what's spinning around in your head in the moment, but it can also inhibit your body's ability to do what it needs to do to sleep. Possible non-screen alternatives may be to read a (paper) book, listen to classical music, or snuggle the family pet, though these also can be distractions that continue to prevent sleep from coming. If you do intend to read, be mindful of lighting and noise and how it may affect your circadian rhythm and the sleep of your partner.

But if you do decide you need to get out of bed, do so with the assurance that you are not alone in the night. Then, with that hope before you, and with the lights off or dimmed, take out your prayer beads (see chapter 4 of this resource). Do some meditation (chapter 3). Put on some relaxing music (chapter 5; I find Gregorian chant helpful). Try some breathing exercises (chapter 13).

If it would be more helpful, turn on a light (task lighting is best, as opposed to full room lighting), and do some journaling (chapter 7), or practice some *lectio divina* (chapter 9). In extreme cases (and if you can do so safely), take a walk around the neighborhood (chapter 4).

When you feel yourself getting sleepy, say a simple "Thank you," and return to bed. Sleep well, enjoying God's presence in your night.

Note: While the occasional sleepless night affects most of us, if sleeplessness is becoming a regular issue for you, consult your medical practitioner or counselor. This is not a failure; it is a confession that we are not alone in the world, and we need the gifts that others possess.

HOLDING SACRED SPACE

What Is It?

Martin Luther described an expression of grace beyond the sacraments, as demonstrated in the "mutual conversation and consolation of believers."[3] In this deepening relationship, we find sacred space. This relationship does not necessarily mean friendship or familial kinship but a spiritual link from our cores.

3. Luther, "Smalcald Articles," specifically no. 4, "Concerning the Gospel," 319.

Space becomes sacred when we honor it for what it is. Engaging in this space between us means that we intentionally reject practicing judgment, we suppress the desire to "fix," and we carefully and prayerfully refuse to make efforts that affect the outcome of the circumstance. It means that we are relinquishing control over a situation and, instead, we offer support as we open our hearts as widely as we can.

It is a spiritual accompaniment, regardless if we agree with the courses of action that the other is taking. As we accompany folks on their journeys, without trying to force them into our pathway, we are holding space for them.

How Do I Do It?

Primarily, we open our hearts and minds to be and present an intentionally safe space and presence.

Share your intention to dwell in that sacred space, where God is present with you.

Engage in a time of self-reflective awareness, to identify your own pre-judgments and preconceptions. Do what you need to do to put these assessments aside for this time.

Practice active listening: silence phones and other devices, create an environment free from interruptions, be aware of nonverbal communications, don't jump to conclusions, don't try to plan a reply while the other is speaking, ask questions for clarification, stay focused, etc.

Acknowledge that some topics are uncomfortable: you can honor the situation by sitting with the discomfort instead of trying to fix it.

Thank the person for trusting you with their story.

Ask what the other person would like as a next step; this leaves agency with them.

Be okay with being imperfect, as no one ever holds space perfectly. However, the experience of truly kind and safe space is rare for many today, so having a useful and kind interaction is a blessing.

PRAYERS OF THE DAY

What Is It?

We are called to pray daily; and within our liturgical resources, we have prayers of the day. These can be about saints of the biblical or modern era or specific dates in the calendar (biblical and Gregorian). These daily topics give us the opportunity to learn more about the history of our faith, and how we have been informed and supported by the people, places, and circumstances over the centuries.

However, many other resources provide a focus of the day, too—it could be a trivia app, a daily desktop calendar of must-see travel locations, or the daily "This day in history" entry on Wikipedia. (For the daring, there is "fact of the day" toilet paper that could be useful!) Whatever it is, that daily focus can be used as a resource for prayer, in areas that may or may not be previously known to you.

Our daily prayers can focus on a saint of the day, or a person of history, or a current affairs news item. They may be focused on any aspect of the definition of a noun (a person, place, or thing); some may choose to focus on each of those areas in their daily prayers.

How Do I Do It?

Select a resource that provides a daily focus.

Spend some time learning about that focus—if it's a place, you can learn about its geography and government, language, and traditions. If it's a person, you can explore their circumstances and the influence they have had. If it's an historical era, you can learn about the issues of the time and the impact they had.

As you do some basic research, remember that there may be new understandings and insights into these topics—what you knew before may no longer be what is taught.

Engage with what you have learned, giving thanks to God for what is new to you.

Ask God to help you better understand situations or circumstances that are unknown by you.

Hold in prayer the people living within that context.

Listen to how God may be calling you to action—are you being invited into a particular ministry as a result of this learning?

PRAYING THE NEWS

What Is It?

> O Lord, how long shall I cry for help,
> and you will not listen?
> Or cry to you "Violence!"
> and you will not save?
> Why do you make me see wrongdoing
> and look at trouble?
> Destruction and violence are before me;
> strife and contention arise.
> So the law becomes slack
> and justice never prevails.
> The wicked surround the righteous—
> therefore judgement comes forth perverted. (Hab 1:2–4)

We watch and/or listen to the news to learn what's happening in our world. Yet, it is easy to become overwhelmed by what we see and hear because there seems no end to the bad. It can be helpful to remember that there are countless good things happening that don't make the news.

Praying the news is a way of *listening* to the news of the day, which helps us remember the presence of God in the midst of it, and a way of *responding* to the news of the day by invoking the presence of God *into* the midst of it.

How Do I Do It?

Watch the news! Listen to the news. Read the news. As hard as it may be (and it can be pretty hard).

At the end of each story (or even in the middle of them), offer a prayer for the people involved. Ask God for insight about the story. Ask God for energy to deal with the ramifications of the story. Pray for the victims in the story; pray for the perpetrators in the story; pray for the bystanders and witnesses; pray for the one who is reporting the story; pray for those who want to ignore the story. Ask where God might be (hidden?) in the story.

Granted, this approach might work best if you are reading news sources (newspapers, magazines, online articles, blogs, etc.) in which you can take a moment to pray, because news broadcasts (TV, radio, cable news, etc.) move on to the next story with no break or pause (unless it's for a commercial, which is anything *but* restful or prayer-friendly!).

That being said, life frequently confronts us with circumstances that do not allow a break or a pause to collect ourselves. In these cases, a simple *Kyrie eleison*, "Lord, have mercy," will be a profound, and profoundly honest, prayer.

Chapter 13

Silent Prayers

SILENCE

What Is It?

Psalm 62 begins with the calming, settling assurance, "For God alone my soul in silence waits; from God comes my salvation." This does not mean that those who are extroverted social butterflies cannot find God or that we would be denied the promise of salvation (phew!); instead, it recognizes that this is one pathway that offers meaningful connection for some.

The prayer of silence is not a proscriptive format as such; rather, it is a pathway for opening oneself to the movement of the Spirit. Trusting that God knows the intention of the silence, our efforts become less important. The effect of the silent prayers will be known in how we exercise our ministry in the rest of our lives, rather than as a set accomplishment during the prayers.

Silent prayers are not merely an absence of noise or an avoidance of talking. Those are auditory receptions of the world working around us. And most of us know how frenetic and noisy life can be. Instead, silent prayers are a time of getting comfortable in an external quietness that provides the context for an internal stillness. In accomplishing the quieted soul within us, we recognize benefits of increased creative expression, perspective, focus, self-awareness, and self-control.

In silent prayers, we aim to reduce the noise of our lives so that we can hear the still, small voice of the Spirit as God whispers to our hearts. This is a temporary setting, intentionally kept to a shorter duration with a defined end (usually beginning with five minutes and gradually increasing to twenty). The practice is one of continual growth and deepening connection with God.

How Do I Do It?

Set a time for your practice. Get comfortable in your chosen space, where you will not be interrupted.

If holding something will calm you, hold it; if you are likely to fidget, having empty hands may be best. Many find peace in sitting with their hands open, palms upward.

Some people close their eyes for silent prayer; however, if this is likely to invite sleep, perhaps this is a better time for physical rest. (Nap ministry is important! Consider Elijah under the broom tree in 1 Kgs 19:4–6 or Jesus in the boat in Matt 8:24.)

A focus item may be helpful (such as a candle, an icon, or a symbol); ensure it will direct you to silence instead of reflection or analysis.

When you begin your silence, be aware of your body: pay attention to the sense of your breathing, your positioning, your comfort.

Feel the tensions release.

A word may be repeated as a mantra to aid in keeping your intention clear. (Some examples may be Jesus or Spirit or Holy.) This word is not the prayer but a conduit to inner peace.

If/when outside or mundane thoughts come, acknowledge them. They are not bad; they just are. This is normal. After acknowledgment, release the thoughts. You do not need to retain them here. (For the thoughts that remain, it can be helpful to write them down. Some people bring a notepad with them to silent prayer for this purpose.)

Remain in the space of silence until your time is ended.

Offer a (word) prayer of gratitude to God for the time, and ask for God's blessing as you return to the rest of your day, carrying the stillness within you.

BREATH PRAYERS

What Is It?

The breath of God is the breath of life; the movement of air in and through us shares the timeless connection we share with the divine. The Scriptures reference the breath of God, the *ruach* (Hebrew for "breath"), in ways that always lead to new life: from the creation receiving that first breath, through prophecies (such as Israel's individual and collection reanimation as new breath enters what was once dry bones in Ezek 37), to Jesus' personal interaction with his disciples distributing peace on his breath (John 20), through the exuberant breath of God on the apostles at the Pentecost (Acts 2). This continues beyond the back cover of the Scriptures into our lives today. Breath is life and health; with each breath, we reconnect to the source of love and life. God's breath not only gives us the promise of new life but widens our potential for healing as individuals, families, communities, and the whole church.

With a focus on breathing, we are grounding ourselves and using breath to enter into prayerful meditative space.

How Do I Do It?

Sit in a comfortable place where you will not be disturbed. Be mindful of those things that are in your mind and heart. If it is helpful to write these things down, do so.

Be aware of your breaths, aiming to breathe deeply into the diaphragm and not just the lungs and stomach. Take time with your breaths, making them deep and slow, and holding for as long as is comfortable and helpful while you reflect.

Start with a few deep breaths just to clear your mind. Some examples are below.

Option One: Alone

Follow a simple pattern of awareness and focus on your breaths. You may use a set collection of words to assist, such as the one offered here:

Breathe in God's love; breathe out any doubts.

Breathe in God's joy; breathe out any sadness.

Breathe in God's peace; breathe out any conflict.

Breathe in God's hope; breathe out any anxieties.

Breathe in God's grace; breathe out feeling only purity in your heart and mind.

Option Two: Group Setting

Seated without touching, we use our breath to re-root ourselves as individuals and as a connected community. Remember throughout the exercise that the power of God's presence is not limited to us alone; it is given to us to be shared, and there is more than enough for all of us to share.

With the first breath, we fuel ourselves; placing a hand over our heart or lungs or any other place where we wish to feel God's presence or healing.

Take a big, deep breath; hold it with a focus on the area where it is wanted.

When you release this breath, do so with intentionality in a hum or big blow, using this exhale to let your body get rid of whatever it needs to.

(Repeat this fueling breath as needed. Sometimes, once just isn't enough!)

In the second phase, consider someone who is with you in the room or in your mind; inhaling with a focus on that person. Ask God to embrace that person as the breath is being held. In your exhalation, remember that God has given you the power of *ruach*, and that you are now sharing that power with the person (or people) of your intention. Eyes can be open or closed, based on comfort level; some may wish to hold up their palms towards the person they are sharing their power with. (This works well in a group video prayer session.)

Repeat this as many times as the Spirit moves.

Chapter 14

Roadblocks and Obstacles

In this section, we are intentionally breaking from the pattern of the previous chapters. This is because the ever-evolving and highly individual reality of obstacles to a fruitful prayer life are not something that can be easily catalogued, nor could we provide every possibility for overcoming them. That being said, we have long known from our own experience that challenges or obstacles along the prayerful journey are normal! They help to inform and influence our growth—and they lead to resilience, persistence, community building, and new engagements with a praying community. So, we name that there will always be roadblocks, but there are also work-arounds that invite us back to that forward motion of prayer. These work-arounds (like the roadblocks themselves) are always evolving, morphing in how we apply them, and providing varying results. What is highly effective in addressing one roadblock may be entirely futile in another; we want to ensure that we all remain encouraged to find whatever means it takes for us to continue living into our connection with the Divine.

LAMENT

What Is It?

We all experience bad days, bad moments. Sadness is a reality. And praying these moments allows us to bring our burdens to God, trusting that we are never alone in the journey. It is for these reasons that Jesus reminds us that when we share these struggles, the yoke becomes easier, and the burden is lightened (Matt 11:30). Jesus never says that the sharing of a burden will make it disappear, but an honest assessment of the load can help us source the right people and tools to travel through those times.

The prayer of lament has a long history; one merely needs to consider the scriptural examples of those who have suffered and who have cried to God for help: Job is often cited (despite his well-intentioned but unhelpful friends) or the Book of Lamentations, to say nothing of Jesus crying out from the cross, "My God, why have you forsaken me?" (quoting Ps 22). These examples allow us to see that approaching God on our bad and sad days is a holy prayer.

Lament is healthy when things are hard. And life is hard; it's a four-letter word, after all. Prayers of lamentation allow us to face the days when we are *not* okay—and to know that it is okay not to be okay. Laments are not seeking quick-fixes or even solutions to our stress. They are identifying something that is denying us the fullness of the abundant life that has been promised us. Lament is normal.

Through these prayers, we address the realities of our present experience—the grief, depression, oppression, devastation, hurt, injustice—whatever is causing distress to our souls, we bring to God.

We are not doing this to dwell in those moments; we don't want to extend them. However, by being present with them, and allowing them to be present with us, we are honoring the harsh realities of being a human and the impact of an imperfect world on ourselves—our minds, our bodies, our souls. We know that when we love, we are opening ourselves up to the possibility of being hurt, and that the risk is well worth the reward. This vulnerability to each other is also healthy and can aid in the process of healing.

When we are hurt, our lamentations allow us to name the issues that weigh upon us, without engaging or enforcing toxic positivity. The gift of lament is to acknowledge our pain and not try to force it away too quickly. Our cultural inclination of always showing a smiling face (which is sometimes unhelpfully reinforced by our faith traditions) can lead to deeper wounds and isolations. Yes, faith looks toward healing, but it recognizes that the first step is to acknowledge the true circumstance in which we find ourselves and embracing the long journey we are making. As with physical wounds, spiritual woundedness requires time to heal, after first stopping the injury/disease from continuing.

For those experiencing extreme distress and unease, we recommend seeking professional assistance. Prayer is a powerful component of healing, but it is not always the only answer. Sometimes medication and counseling, augmented by prayer, is also needed—we say this from our own experiences.

How Do I Do It?

Allow yourself time and space. Lament can bring to the forefront a deeper pain than we may have previously been aware of, and it can take longer than we have scheduled to address it.

Find a place where you can be comfortable and uninterrupted for a period of time.

"Get comfortable with being uncomfortable." Healing is a painful process (ask anyone recovering from surgery or undergoing physiotherapy).

Allow yourself to feel. Allow yourself to feel *deeply*.

Name the pain. Keeping track of your emotions can be helpful; a private journal can record the challenges. These journals can be helpful in the process as you can look back for trends and cycles—and hopefully recognize a healing trajectory. (On a bad day, it feels like they have all been bad days, but the number or duration of bad days may in fact be decreasing).

Tell God how you are feeling. God wants us to be honest with ourselves and with God; after all, God has gifted us with the ability to feel these emotions, so that we can learn from them.

Ideally, if you have someone with whom you can be vulnerable, ask if they are able to share the journey with you. They may not be; and for someone to discern they are not equipped is not a rejection of your trusted request but an honest and respectful awareness of their own limitations.

When you are ready (when the tears stop, when you simply can't go further, if it feels like enough for now), take a deep breath, and let your extended exhalation be a breath of thanks for God's presence with you in the middle of your challenges.

Note: We all feel "blue" occasionally. But if you notice yourself feeling "stuck" in that mindset, please consult your medical practitioner or counsellor. This is not a lack of faith; it is welcoming, and even embracing, the fact that we need the gifts which other people can offer.

DRY SPELLS

There are any number of reasons why a dry spell can happen in our prayer life: busy schedules, unexpected obligations, a disrupted day, week, or month. For example, while prayer definitely happens in schools during exams, the period of exam preparation may reallocate prayer time in a lower priority space. An unexpected workload, like a work project with a short timeline, may again interrupt our prayerful patterns. Schedules are often disrupted during holiday or vacation time (I know I don't carry along my prayer resources when on a backwoods camping trip).

These types of disruptions can be easily remedied when things return to "normal" (or a new normal is created); yet, for some, they can also begin an unfortunate new pattern where prayer is not a priority. This leads to a dry spell caused by a non-crisis.

At other times, experiences of tragedy or stress may cause our faith to falter and our prayer practice to wane. This can thus become a cyclical diminishment: as prayer decreases and our intentionality wanes, so, too, does a sense of the faith that sustains us. These events can be similar to those identified above, whereby the disruption of pattern and norms is enough to dislodge the pattern of prayer. However, they may also be influenced by the precipitant cause itself—a sudden illness, a tragedy, a devastation of heart—these can all bring on the normal sense of being disconnected or disfavored by God, leading to a path of disconnection and an end to prayer. Sometimes, these stresses can be considered as a conflict with God, and thus, the lack of prayerful connection is a result of that (misplaced) anger.

Regardless, these dry spells are less of a situational circumstance, and it can take a lot longer to emerge into a place of remedy and reconciliation. As with any relationship, breakdowns in trust and communication are problematic, and it can take a lot of work on all sides to rebuild that respect and interconnection. Even more so when one cannot participate in activities focused on communication building between individuals, such as attending therapy or mediation with God as partner, the restoration of relationship can be difficult.

Another way to enter into a dry spell is simply to sense that the time spent in prayer is not beneficial. A spiritual ennui can be dangerous, as there does not seem to be a particular root cause to address. Likewise, a sense of disconnect from God can make one feel unheard, unappreciated, and abandoned. Feeling alone, like prayer is merely speaking into a void, can be not only destabilizing but demoralizing.

In an age where we are more and more focused on our accomplishments and "efficient" use of time (time being considered a resource), a lack of perceiving "successful" results from prayer can make it easy to walk away. Concepts of "success" and "efficiency" are culturally influenced (if not outright dictated), and in our society, which seeks and values instant gratification, it can be a major challenge to do anything long term. The call in prayer is persistence with much patience. We are in a relationship with God, and prayer is the lifelong process of developing that relationship. It can be challenging to let it take as long as it takes, but we believe that's what we are called to do.

Our spirits cannot drink deeply from a well that they cannot even find, let alone pull water from. The thirst for genuine connection may not always be sated by what is received. And just because a previous experience has been nourishing and life-giving does not mean that same practice will always result in a similar experience (for we are people with different perspectives every day, depending on what is going on around us). A dry spell can be a break from prayer, a sense that prayer is not fulfilling, or a rejection of prayer as it feels useless.

Discerning the root cause of the dry spell is important in addressing our response to it; as dry spells are intersected with other aspects of our lives. And, as with all areas that are woven together, all areas need to eventually be addressed.

That being said, it is helpful to remember that dry spells are normal; every well will run dry from time to time. This is where our experience and companions can benefit our reengagement, as we acknowledge that a dry spell does not mean a perpetual dryness; dry wells can be refilled.

Continuing the practice of prayer in a spiritual dry spell is an act of hope and trust—a commitment to restoration of spiritual health. Returning from the dry spell may feel ambivalent if one is merely saying the words (which feel empty); yet, this practice is an incredibly important aspect. In doing so, the words or actions become part of our memory again; they help to reestablish our habits to include space for the sacred to seep in. Using the well analogy, repeating the words of prayer demonstrates that our spirits know where to go to seek that refreshing water, how to access it, and drink deeply from it.

Martin Thornton (mentioned previously) celebrates the integral nature of prayer to all aspects of our lives. His theology invites us to appreciate that nature, recognizing five basic principles: 1) prayer is to be embraced while recognizing our desired outcome is not promised; 2) a structured prayerful life is not legalistic or restrictive but intended to be liberating and responsive to our lives; 3) prayer is not to be artificial, nor a burden, but to enhance our Christian life; 4) missing our intended prayer practices or structure is not sinful but part of the human condition; and 5) prayer is always variable in life, as life is seldom without change. Each person is invited to establish and follow (and regularly reevaluate) a rule of life (or *regula*), which can help overcome the desperation of dry spells and minimize their challenging impact on our spiritual journeys.[1]

The structured practices that sustain us also serve to benefit others in our midst. Religion can be considered as a chain of memory, the links of which are weakened or even broken when individuals (or families, communities, even society as a whole) forget the benefits of a spiritual life and, thus, rest in a type of spiritual amnesia.

Social scientist Danièle Hervieu-Léger considers how religion is passed from generation to generation through a type of chain of memory, as with so many other aspects of our lives. She argues that the future of religion relies on the collective body to maintain the shared memory, which in turn provides both a collective responsibility and a collective benefit.[2]

Whether the desire for increased spirituality is individual or societal, one may tap into that collective memory of consistent prayer practices that are well-established within the community. They offer us the depth, structure, and accountability that is necessary for the health of the prayer practice (and the practitioner). This can prevent prayers being self-serving or individualistic, instead becoming intentionally rooted and grounded in the traditions, social links, and collective validation that make the experience authentic.

Recognizing a dry spell is an important first step, not as a matter of shame or blame but as a means to engage what is going on in our interior. As referenced above, there are any number of factors that may be contributing to that spiritual dryness.

A time of intentional reflection and discernment can be essential in the process of coming through a dry spell. (They are very seldom broken in an immediate sense; they take time and effort to overcome, and the best chance of success comes when root causes have at least been identified.)

1. Thornton, *Pastoral Theology.*

2. Hervieu-Léger, *Chain of Memory.*

Finding out why we are experiencing a dry spell can help us understand what tools we will need to repair our wells, or to find a new one altogether.

One of the practices to begin to counter a dry spell that is both easiest and most difficult is pray. This is not the time for ground-breaking creativity or ingenuity; it is a reminder of the practice and ritual of prayer.

See, for example, the section on the Lord's Prayer in chapter 8. Many people find it helpful to have a prayer memorized and/or familiar so they don't have to think too much about it, especially when we are in the middle of challenging times. Also, as mentioned above, praying a prayer that we know others are praying can be a source of support as we wander our own wildernesses. In prayer, we are never alone.

It may also be helpful simply to surround ourselves with praying people. Attending a church service can be of benefit, not as an instant fix but as a means to immerse ourselves in the prayerful space and experience. Just as one can learn a language best by being surrounded by it, so, too, will we open ourselves to that comfortable space of prayer by allowing ourselves to be entirely within it.

Another key component to countering the effects of dry spells is to speak to someone about the dry spell itself. If you have a prayer partner or prayer team or spiritual director or clergyperson, you can approach them with your reality. Most often, we expect to hear of our doubt or dry spell as a weakness or failure; yet, these trusted companions are likely going to be nonjudgmental, supportive, and appreciate your willingness to be vulnerable. They may be helpful with the causes and effects of your circumstance, and if they are not, they should be able to direct you to appropriate counsel.

Realistically, dry spells are more common than we think (or than we'd like to think); yet, grace abounds. The dryness is part of the journey.

NOPE!: RESISTANCE TO PRAYER

There are many times when something within us resists prayer; it can be an external factor, a general malaise, an internal struggle, a spiritual crisis. When we find ourselves resisting prayer, we do ourselves a favor by spending time and energy to understand the root cause.

There are a couple of distinctions we are going to make for this section. There is resistance *to* prayer, and there is resistance *in* prayer. These need a different analysis and assessment, and addressing these resistances can look very differently. Sometimes these overlap, and that can amplify the confusion around discerning what is going on within our prayer journey.

We want to clarify that resistance is not a bad thing; it is not a state to be ashamed of or to be considered a failure. In fact, the best thing we can do in that moment is admit our reluctance. That itself is a prayer and is a step toward healing.

Besides, when we are in tune with our prayer life, we know that it is relational. Just as with any relationship, our connection with God will have ebbs and flows as we journey along. Life happens; our prayers will reflect that.

Resistance *to* Prayer

Let's be honest: sometimes, we simply don't want to pray. There may be any number of reasons for this. We, ourselves, have experienced some of the following.

We might have some connection to a negative emotion or experience, and we are aiming to avoid that happening again. For example, if someone had a bad experience with one format of prayer, they are likely to avoid that altogether in the future. Even considering a different format or system of prayer can be intimidating, as it evokes the core emotional reaction to whatever it was that caused pain. This reluctance then amplifies the natural hesitancy to try something new.

There might be a traumatic event in our past that we associate with prayer. A friend, who lived in a wheelchair, was once told that if she prayed the "right way" and "really believed," God would enable her to get out of the wheelchair and walk. She really tried, but she ended up flat on the ground, bruised and shaken. Understandably, it took her a long time to recognize that prayer could be a positive part of her life again.

Another friend admitted once that she didn't want to pray because she was afraid of what God might ask her to do. And this concern isn't necessarily wrong! Our hearts may be guided, our actions may be influenced, our journeys may be changed based on what we think or suspect that God may ask of us. In doing this (rather like sticking our fingers in our ears), we refuse to acknowledge the potential for change and, thus, are not responsible for making the adjustments or changes in our lives.

Another type of avoidance/resistance can occur when we have had an exceptional time of prayer; knowing that we are unlikely to have a repeat of such a mountaintop experience (and not wanting to be disappointed by prayer), we opt to avoid prayer altogether, as it will no longer live up to our expectations. This "all or nothing" mentality can create reluctance, as the extreme high may be idealized in hindsight and remembered as even better than it was . . . thereby increasing the gap between our romanticized version of what was and the ordinariness of what is.

Resistance *in* Prayer

At times, our prayers may provide insights and wisdom that is well beyond our comfort zone; this depth may become a barrier to going further, until we have had ample time to comprehend this new awareness and its implications on our lives. As the saying goes, we learn to walk before we learn to run; so, too, with the depth of our prayers. In this case, our resistance is a positive experience, as we are taking the new understanding seriously and doing our best to fully appreciate and apply it to our lives.

We may also be stuck in our own experience and are not yet able to consider a prayerful response, and so we resist the conversation altogether until we are ready and able. I recall a time in my early formation when I was angry at earthly circumstances; without an accessible target, I directed that anger to God—each day I would wake and stubbornly blurt out, "I'm not talking to you!" like a petulant teenager. As my anger eased and my inner hurt healed, I realized that even in my declaration of non-communication, I was communicating: I was just doing so within the parameters that worked for me at the time. I later recognized that God had always listened, patiently, to my angry prayer, accepting it for what it was, and accompanied me until I was on the other side of my anger; and thus, we engaged in a new and renewed relationship.

In our prayers, sometimes we hit an area of resistance that is subtle or nuanced, and we don't understand why; yet, we also realize that we cannot move past it. This may be when prayer feels too overwhelming or too difficult, or when we put up intentional roadblocks or limitations (without seeking out alternative routes), or asking others to pray for us (not on our behalf but in our stead), as we are feeling too much of a primary emotion (fear, anger, sadness, joy), or if we feel prayer is no longer meaningful for us, or if we are feeling too ashamed for authentic communication with God.

Addressing Resistance

Whatever the cause of our resistance, we benefit from learning more about what's causing it. This can be worked through with a trusted spiritual advisor or director. Resistance isn't unholy; it's an opportunity to deepen our relationship with the Divine, and this allows us the privilege of learning more about ourselves in our spiritual journey. In overcoming resistance to prayer, we overcome the instinctive, reactive part of ourselves—the lizard brain. And while our minds may protest ("But I like my lizard brain!"), we also want to grow and develop in our spirituality and faithfulness in prayer.

In exploring our resistance, we also can explore alternative options for working through the pause. Prayer may force us to go where we don't want to go, but it never forces us beyond where we *can* go—for prayer is holy ground, and God will never leave us alone or unsupported.

Taking a break from prayer is recognizing that prayer (as a longing of the soul) is happening without our words and that our present circumstances and practices are just not aligned at this time. This realization, then, shows that a break from prayer is, in fact, another form of prayer that is nudging and inviting us into a deeper and more meaningful relationship of prayer.

When we are recognizing our spiritual dryness, we return to prayer; sometimes, the same familiar words will feed our souls in ways we are not expecting; sometimes, trying a new style or manner of prayer will engage a compartment of our spirit that we didn't even know was there. These efforts may work for us, or they may feel empty or ineffective; each experience will need time for reflection and evaluation (and possibly trying again!). The importance is in the genuine attempt to continue in relationship.

The gift of prayer—in its many expressions and experiences, its floods and its droughts, our keenness and our resistance—is all a way of recognizing and celebrating the movement of the Spirit in our lives. For the Spirit is an outside-the-box thinker, spreading blessings with reckless abandon through all forms of connection, lavishing grace upon grace at every opportunity. The Spirit will not, and cannot, be contained, and our willingness to return to the practice of prayer in whatever form honors the movement of the Spirit in our lives.

PRAYER GONE WRONG

At one point in my life, I believed that there was no wrong way to pray.

I was wrong!

For I have encountered any number of prayers that did not fully embrace the grace and blessing that is the gift of prayer. In prayer, God already knows the intentions of our hearts, and it takes a spiritual maturity to ensure that our words and actions align with the faith we profess. It is tempting to tell God exactly what we expect and to claim a particular outcome; yet, this practice does not follow sound theology. Even Jesus deferred to the Father when it came to prayer: "Then he withdrew from them about a stone's throw, knelt down, and prayed, 'Father, if you are willing, remove this cup from me; yet, not my will but yours be done'" (Luke 22:41–42).

The phenomena of prayer gone wrong is not new; it is not unique to our modern world. The psalms are full of examples that can, and do, shock us as we hear what has been written as holy requests. For example, Ps 137:8–9 reads,

> O daughter Babylon, you devastator!
> Happy shall they be who pay you back
> what you have done to us!
> Happy shall they be who take your little ones
> and dash them against the rock!

Such expression is, quite frankly, denying the potential of sacred conversation; it is a primal and very human bloodlust coming from a desperate and devastated circumstance. While it is not wrong to admit that sometimes our base desires get the best of our thoughts, we must be careful that we don't speak those as intentions or expectations—lest someone record them for the ages and misunderstand our intended connection with community.

Here, we do our best to identify some of the ways that we have seen prayer gone wrong—and that we do our very best to avoid and mitigate.

Idolatry

We must be careful when we tell God what we want, for this is when prayer ceases to be a conversation seeking connection and guidance from God and, instead, it serves as a wish list or set of demands. By making this encounter a one-way conversation, prayer becomes what a friend calls "cosmic mail." To be fair, there is nothing wrong with a wish list being released into the universe, but the wisher needs to remember that it is just that: a wish. To have the expectation that all our wishes will be granted—as we wish them to be—is naive and unhelpful and can lead to a slippery slope towards idolatry.

When a wish/prayer is not answered the way we have expected/demanded, this can have painful consequences. It can become unhealthy, when wishes do not come true, to consider that to be a failure of the prayer, of themselves, or even of God. It can be spiritually damaging for a leader to promise that praying "hard enough" will make everything turn out according to our own will (rather than finding our way within God's will). Praying for our earthly benefit may mean someone else's earthly suffering; and praying for our personal gain may in fact take us to that place of inadvertently expecting God to provide all that the devil tempted Christ with in the wilderness.

Hearing "no" can be difficult, be it for earthly desires or prayerful pleas. It takes time and patience to try and seek the blessing in the "no," and sometimes we don't. Here is an example: as a child, I wished for a pony. My (nonreligious) parents told me to pray for it, which I did. I never got the pony. And while this saddened me at the time, as an adult, I can respect and appreciate it: we moved often, we lived in suburbs with small yards, we had no experience with livestock, and we never had the financial resources to care for a pony. Had my wish/prayer been answered as I desired, it would have been bad for the pony, for me, for my family, for our neighbors . . . the "no" was the correct answer, I just couldn't see it at the time.

This doesn't mean my prayer was wrong, or ignored, or unanswered—quite the opposite. I believe that God hears all of our prayers and journeys with us as we come to understand *how* they are answered and how we can apply that to our growth as praying people.

"For prayer is request. The essence of request, as distinct from compulsion, is that it may or may not be granted."[3]

Gossip

Prayers can also go wrong when we misuse the privilege of praying with and for others. We have heard of times where people have shared inappropriate information, and they have inadvertently broken confidences; in some instances, they have used a time of prayer to spread gossip (for

3. Lewis, "Efficacy of Prayer," in *World's Last Night*, 6.

whatever psychological benefit one might receive from such activity). At times, prayer can come dangerously close to (and sometimes cross the line of) matters of domination and control (of individuals or communities), social isolation or ostracism from the community, blatant judgment and criticism, promoting a personal agenda, or forcing an imposition of views.

Prayer goes wrong when the intention of the heart of the one praying is not for God's will to be done but for their own personal benefit.

Manipulation

Praying to ask God to change someone else, in order to try and force them to be more like ourselves, may not be the most helpful act. In doing so, we are creating a deity who we expect to do our will, rather than trusting God to be God. When these prayers are spoken aloud, it can act as a means to coerce or manipulate the praying community and/or the focus of the prayer being vocalized.

Condescension

A prime example of this is "I'll pray for you!" This phrase does not always carry with it the positive, affirming reality that one would hope for. Instead, those words can be burdened with a weight of condescension, not unlike multifaceted meanings of "Bless your heart." This simple phrase, if misused, is a conduit for the negative and self-serving aspects listed above, thus making the words a threat or an insult. Less offensively, "I'll pray for you" can be a presumptive statement, if one has not felt heard in communicating their desires and petitions. It can also be an overstepping, if the person sharing news is merely sharing news and is not requesting prayers. This can be painful if the person is not a person of faith, or is of a different faith, and thus, the promise of prayers can feel like an unfamiliar or uncomfortable religious imposition.

Deflection

Similarly, the phrase "I'll pray for you" is one that we say regularly, yet should give us pause, for the promise to pray is not a casual comment to be lightly stated to offer immediate comfort. A lack of engagement is strongly discouraged after such a promise has been made! These few short words convey a commitment to undertake this sacred intention: to purposefully and faithfully pray for someone else to the best of our ability. It is a ministry and a gift—and one we ought to take seriously.

Addressing Prayer Gone Wrong

It can be intimidating to counter a prayer gone wrong; and so often, merely removing oneself from the situation can show disconnect from intentional negativity under false prayers, or gently speaking with the prayer-giver if there has been unintentional harm. Thus, prevention of such prayers through our own example can be helpful and aid in building up best practices within a praying community.

The best way to avoid prayer gone wrong is to be intentional about how we pray, and this includes carefully determining the comfort and consent of the people we are praying with and for. "How can I pray for you?" is a simple question that grants the control of the circumstance to those individuals and respects their dignity and decisions. It further invites them to deeply consider their own stance in the praying experience, which ultimately leads to a healthier experience for all.

Avoiding "prayer gone wrong" can be a struggle; but the struggle itself can be beautiful and rewarding as we grow toward a healthy balance in prayer.

Conclusion: Amen Is not the End

While we have been collaborating on this book for some time, there have been countless numbers of ups and downs in our lives, with copious changes (some expected, some surprising, some minor, some dramatic!). We have moved, we have changed ministries, we have experienced the world in ways we could not have imagined when we began this adventure. There has been more coffee and cola consumed than our doctors would likely advise; there has been laughter so hard our stomachs ached and tears after our hearts have broken.

Life has happened.

And throughout this, we have continued to deepen and strengthen our resolve both to the prayer that sustains us and the knowledge and articulation of the role of prayer in our lives.

We believe that prayer is the privilege and responsibility of the faithful: regardless of location, denomination, ordination, time, situation. . . . If you can think, you can pray. If you can speak, you can pray. If you can feel, you can pray.

Part of our call, as people who wrestle with prayer, is to communicate that all of us (the faithful people, the seeking people, the questioning people, the people who have turned away from faith) are praying more than we realize. The difference arises in how much we can recognize and be aware of prayer. Intentionality is a contributing factor, of course, but we are always in connection with God. And our prayer is responding to the fact that God is always in connection with us!

Some of the prayer formats that we have offered in this booklet look and *are* recreational. This is not because it's just fun to do (though it is!) but because, in recreation, we are participating in the recreation of ourselves.

God loved us into being, as created and creating beings, meant to demonstrate love in all things. Yet, the challenges of life can intervene, and our creativity can diminish; and so, when we reconnect to that part of ourselves, we are honoring the recreated and recreating the gift of being remade in the image of God.

The more formalized expressions of prayer that we have offered are not meant to be contradictory to this celebration of creativity; instead, they are offered as a calming presence, a haven and idyll for many. Many seek the stillness and find within it what they need to feel themselves recreated in love. By gently disengaging from the busyness and business of the world to dedicate time and heart to prayer, the practice of prayer allows the one praying to find (tended within their being) that image of God deep within.

The image of God, or *imago Dei*, doesn't mean that we have the physical attributes to match those of an anthropomorphized divinity; it means that we bear in our very being the image of God's love. It is through the gift of our connection with God that we are able to bear an authentic image for the world to see, and that connection *is* prayer. Even on a micro level, just as our cells continue to re-form in our bodies, our spiritual growth and development re-form in our beings, such that the prayer we dwell in can offer us all that we need to love and see God in all the world.

Through prayer, we resist the distractions of the world that would take us away from being the loving people Jesus calls us to be. Through prayer, we acknowledge that we are on the precipice of the work that God has for us in the world. Prayer allows us to be *in* the task-oriented world but not *of* the unending to-do-lists of the world, and thus, we move past seeing prayer as a "job" or "duty" into experiencing it as being in communion (not just communication) with the divine.

Prayer is, of course, a response to a relationship; yet, we have also come to trust that it can also *be* the actual relationship.

We have enjoyed this time of prayerful writing and hope that you have found this supportive of your own relationship with God—where "amen" is never the end.

Appendix 1

THIS IS AN EXAMPLE of a stations devotion—this one recounting the story of the Epiphany (the visit of the magi to the child Jesus).

As noted in chapter 9, this may be prayed in a community or on one's own. The following has been formatted for a community setting (normal font for the leader, italics for the community), but this is by no means exclusive. Pray as it is appropriate or as it is possible.

A Light in the Darkness;
A Light to the Nations
A Devotion for the Festival of the Epiphany
in Fourteen Stations
Written in 2007 by Rick Pryce

OPENING PRAYERS

In the name of the Father, the Son, and the Holy Spirit.
Amen.
Lord, have mercy.
Lord, have mercy.
Christ, have mercy.
Christ, have mercy.
Lord, have mercy.
Lord, have mercy.
Our Father in heaven, hallowed be your name.
Your kingdom come, your will be done on earth as in heaven.
Give us today our daily bread,

and forgive us our sins as we forgive those who sin against us.
Save us from the time of trial, and deliver us from evil.
For the kingdom, the power, and the glory are yours,
now and forever. Amen.

Arise, shine; for your light has come,
And the glory of the Lord has risen upon you.

STATION ONE: A LIGHT TO THE NATIONS

The light shines in the darkness.
And the darkness did not overtake it.

"Now the Lord said to Abram, 'Go from your country and your kindred and your father's house to the land that I will show you. I will make of you a great nation, and I will bless you and make your name great, so that you will be a blessing. I will bless those who bless you, and the one who curses you I will curse, and in you all the families of the earth shall be blessed'" (Gen 12:1–3).

"And now the Lord says, who formed me in the womb to be his servant, to bring Jacob back to him, and that Israel might be gathered to him, for I am honored in the sight of the Lord, and my God has become my strength—he says, 'It is too light a thing that you should be my servant to raise up the tribes of Jacob and to restore the survivors of Israel; I will give you as a light to the nations, that my salvation may reach to the end of the earth'" (Isa 49:5–6).

[*Silence for personal reflection*]

"Let the peoples praise you, O God;
Let all the peoples praise you" (Ps 67:3).

God who shines on us and in us, your promises encompass more than we can imagine and take us to places we cannot anticipate. Open us to all that you are bringing, that our lives may reflect your loving-kindness, through Jesus Christ our Lord.
Amen.

STATION TWO: MAGI SEARCH FOR THE CHILD

The light shines in the darkness.
And the darkness did not overtake it.

"In the time of King Herod, after Jesus was born in Bethlehem of Judea, magi from the east came to Jerusalem, asking, 'Where is the child who has been born king of the Jews? For we observed his star in the east and have come to pay him homage'" (Matt 2:1–2).

"Arise, shine, for your light has come, and the glory of the Lord has risen upon you. For darkness shall cover the earth and thick darkness the peoples, but the Lord will arise upon you, and his glory will appear over you. Nations shall come to your light and kings to the brightness of your dawn" (Isa 60:1–3).

[*Silence for personal reflection*]

"Praise is due to you, O God, in Zion, and to you shall vows be performed,

"*O you who answer prayer! To you all flesh shall come*" (Ps 65:1–2).

God who shines on us and in us, lead us, as you led the magi, into unexpected sacred places and holy moments. May all our senses be open to your gracious presence, through Jesus Christ our Lord.

Amen.

STATION THREE: HEROD RESPONDS WITH FEAR

The light shines in the darkness.

And the darkness did not overtake it.

"When King Herod heard this, he was frightened, and all Jerusalem with him" (Matt 2:3).

"Fools say in their hearts, 'There is no God.' They are corrupt; they do abominable deeds; there is no one who does good. . . . Have they no knowledge, all the evildoers who eat up my people as they eat bread and do not call upon the Lord? There they shall be in great terror, for God is with the company of the righteous. You would confound the plans of the poor, but the Lord is their refuge" (Ps 14:1, 4–6).

[*Silence for personal reflection*]

"According to their way I will deal with them; according to their own judgments I will judge them.

"*And they shall know that I am the Lord*" (Ezek 7:27).

God who shines on us and in us, your promise challenges the power and authority of all who rule, and calls us all to the justice of your reign. May we discern your call in this moment and respond for the sake of the world, through Jesus Christ our Lord.

Amen.

STATION FOUR: MESSIAH TO COME FROM BETHLEHEM

The light shines in the darkness.

And the darkness did not overtake it.

"Calling together all the chief priests and scribes of the people, he inquired of them where the Messiah was to be born. They told him, 'In Bethlehem of Judea, for so it has been written by the prophet: "And you, Bethlehem, in the land of Judah, are by no means least among the rulers of Judah, for from you shall come a ruler who is to shepherd my people Israel"'" (Matt 2:4–6). "For surely I know the plans I have for you, says the Lord, plans for your welfare and not for harm, to give you a future with hope. Then when you call upon me and come and pray to me, I will hear you. When you search for me, you will find me" (Jer 29:11–13a).

[*Silence for personal reflection*]

"Do not be afraid, little flock,

for it is your Father's good pleasure to give you the kingdom" (Luke 12:32).

God who shines on us and in us, your word illuminates life, bringing both challenge and promise. Give us the wisdom to listen for your voice and the faith to take the next step, through Jesus Christ our Lord.

Amen.

STATION FIVE: HEROD SENDS THE MAGI TO BETHLEHEM

The light shines in the darkness.

And the darkness did not overtake it.

"Then Herod secretly called for the magi and learned from them the exact time when the star had appeared. Then he sent them to Bethlehem, saying, 'Go and search diligently for the child, and when you have found him, bring me word so that I may also go and pay him homage'" (Matt 2:7–8).

"Transgression speaks to the wicked deep in their hearts; there is no fear of God before their eyes. For they flatter themselves in their own eyes that their iniquity cannot be found out and hated. The words of their mouths are mischief and deceit; they have ceased to act wisely and do good. They plot mischief while on their beds; they are set on a way that is not good; they do not reject evil" (Ps 36:1–4).

[Silence for personal reflection]

"Hide me from the secret plots of the wicked,

from the scheming of evildoers" (Ps 64:2).

God who shines on us and in us, by your coming in the Christ child, you renew all creation. Inspire in us both gratitude and courage, that we, too, may be renewed, through Jesus Christ our Lord.

Amen.

STATION SIX: THE MAGI FOLLOW THE STAR

The light shines in the darkness.

And the darkness did not overtake it.

"When they had heard the king, they set out, and there, ahead of them, went the star that they had seen in the east, until it stopped over the place where the child was. When they saw that the star had stopped, they were overwhelmed with joy" (Matt 2:9–10).

"O send out your light and your truth; let them lead me; let them bring me to your holy hill and to your dwelling. Then I will go to the altar of God, to God my exceeding joy, and I will praise you with the harp, O God, my God" (Ps 43:3–4).

[Silence for personal reflection]

"The heavens are telling the glory of God,

and the firmament proclaims his handiwork" (Ps 19:1).

God who shines on us and in us, the simple sparkle of starlight proclaims your presence and love. Increase our joy in the gift of our being, that we may embrace the journey to which you call us, through Jesus Christ our Lord.

Amen.

STATION SEVEN: GIFTS ARE OFFERED TO JESUS

The light shines in the darkness.

And the darkness did not overtake it.

"On entering the house, they saw the child with Mary his mother, and they knelt down and paid him homage. Then, opening their treasure chests, they offered him gifts of gold, frankincense, and myrrh" (Matt 2:11).

"Lift up your eyes and look around; they all gather together; they come to you; your sons shall come from far away, and your daughters shall be carried in their nurses' arms. Then you shall see and be radiant; your heart shall thrill and rejoice, because the abundance of the sea shall be brought to you; the wealth of the nations shall come to you" (Isa 60:4–5).

[*Silence for personal reflection*]

"Worthy is the Lamb that was slaughtered

to receive power and wealth and wisdom and might and honor and glory and blessing!" (Rev 5:12).

God who shines on us and in us, you provide all we need and more. Grant us a generous spirit, that our sharing may point the world to your abundance, through Jesus Christ our Lord.

Amen.

STATION EIGHT: THE MAGI RETURN HOME

The light shines in the darkness.

And the darkness did not overtake it.

"And having been warned in a dream not to return to Herod, they left for their own country by another road" (Matt 2:12).

"Lead me, O Lord, in your righteousness because of my enemies; make your way straight before me. For there is no truth in their mouths; their hearts are destruction; their throats are open graves; they flatter with their tongues. Make them bear their guilt, O God; let them fall by their own counsels; because of their many transgressions, cast them out, for they have rebelled against you. But let all who take refuge in you rejoice; let them ever sing for joy. Spread your protection over them, so that those who love your name may exult in you. For you bless the righteous, O Lord; you cover them with favor as with a shield" (Ps 5:8–12).

[*Silence for personal reflection*]

"The Lord is good to all,

and his compassion is over all that he has made" (Ps 145:9).

God who shines on us and in us, our paths are not always straight; our destination is frequently a mystery. Send your Spirit, not only to guide but to assure us of your presence on the way, through Jesus Christ our Lord.

Amen.

STATION NINE: AN ANGEL WARNS JOSEPH TO FLEE

The light shines in the darkness.

And the darkness did not overtake it.

"Now after they had left, an angel of the Lord appeared to Joseph in a dream and said, 'Get up, take the child and his mother, and flee to Egypt, and remain there until I tell you, for Herod is about to search for the child, to destroy him.' Then Joseph got up, took the child and his mother by night, and went to Egypt and remained there until the death of Herod. This was to fulfill what had been spoken by the Lord through the prophet, 'Out of Egypt I have called my son'" (Matt 2:13–15).

"Deliver me, O Lord, from evildoers; protect me from those who are violent, who plan evil things in their minds and stir up wars continually. They make their tongue sharp as a snake's, and under their lips is the venom of vipers. *Selah* Guard me, O Lord, from the hands of the wicked; protect me from the violent who have planned my downfall" (Ps 140:1–4).

[*Silence for personal reflection*]

"The Lord answer you in the day of trouble!

The name of the God of Jacob protect you!" (Ps 20:1).

God who shines on us and in us, direct our faltering steps, that we may be protected from despair and discover your guidance in our wanderings, through Jesus Christ our Lord.

Amen.

STATION TEN: HEROD KILLS THE CHILDREN OF BETHLEHEM

The light shines in the darkness.

And the darkness did not overtake it.

"When Herod saw that he had been tricked by the magi, he was infuriated, and he sent and killed all the children in and around Bethlehem who were two years old or under, according to the time that he had learned from the magi. Then what had been spoken through the prophet Jeremiah was fulfilled: 'A voice was heard in Ramah, wailing and loud lamentation, Rachel weeping for her children; she refused to be consoled, because they are no more'" (Matt 2:16–18).

"The precious children of Zion, worth their weight in fine gold—how they are reckoned as earthen pots, the work of a potter's hands!" (Lam 4:2).

[*Silence for personal reflection*]

"Rise up, O Lord; O God, lift up your hand;

do not forget the oppressed" (Ps 10:12).

God who shines on us and in us, the voices of the voiceless cry out to you. Fire us with a desire for your compassionate justice and establish your reign in us, through Jesus Christ our Lord.

Amen.

STATION ELEVEN: JOSEPH RETURNS THE FAMILY TO ISRAEL

The light shines in the darkness.

And the darkness did not overtake it.

"When Herod died, an angel of the Lord suddenly appeared in a dream to Joseph in Egypt and said, 'Get up, take the child and his mother, and go to the land of Israel, for those who were seeking the child's life are dead.' Then Joseph got up, took the child and his mother, and went to the land of Israel" (Matt 2:19–21).

"'Because the poor are despoiled, because the needy groan, I will now rise up,' says the Lord; 'I will place them in the safety for which they long.' The promises of the Lord are promises that are pure, silver refined in a furnace on the ground, purified seven times. You, O Lord, will protect us; you will guard us from this generation forever" (Ps 12:5–7).

[*Silence for personal reflection*]

"The Lord upholds all who are falling

and raises up all who are bowed down" (Ps 145:14).

God who shines on us and in us, restore hope in us, that we, like Joseph, may go where we need to go, trusting the presence of the one who comes with us, Jesus Christ our Lord.

Amen.

STATION TWELVE: JOSEPH MAKES THEIR HOME IN NAZARETH

The light shines in the darkness.

And the darkness did not overtake it.

"Deliver me from my enemies, O my God; protect me from those who rise up against me. Deliver me from those who work evil; from the bloodthirsty, save me. Even now they lie in wait for my life; the mighty stir up strife against me. For no transgression or sin of mine, O Lord, for no fault of mine, they run and make ready" (Ps 59:1–4).

"But when he heard that Archelaus was ruling Judea in place of his father Herod, he was afraid to go there. And after being warned in a dream, he went away to the district of Galilee. There he made his home in a town called Nazareth, so that what had been spoken through the prophets might be fulfilled, 'He will be called a Nazarene'" (Matt 2:22–23).

[*Silence for personal reflection*]

"May God continue to bless us;

let all the ends of the earth revere him" (Ps 67:7).

God who shines on us and in us, calm our restless imaginations with the assurance of your presence, and give us the confidence to go where you lead, through Jesus Christ our Lord.

Amen.

STATION THIRTEEN: A LIGHT TO THE NATIONS

The light shines in the darkness.

And the darkness did not overtake it.

"Thus says God, the Lord, who created the heavens and stretched them out, who spread out the earth and what comes from it, who gives breath to the people upon it and spirit to those who walk in it: 'I am the Lord; I have called you in righteousness; I have taken you by the hand and kept you; I have given you as a covenant to the people, a light to the nations, to open the eyes that are blind, to bring out the prisoners from the dungeon, from the prison those who sit in darkness'" (Isa 42:5–7).

"Sing and rejoice, O daughter Zion! For I will come and dwell in your midst, says the Lord. Many nations shall join themselves to the Lord on that day and shall be my people, and I will dwell in your midst. And you shall know that the Lord of hosts has sent me to you" (Zech 2:10–11).

[*Silence for personal reflection*]

"Be still, and know that I am God!

I am exalted among the nations; I am exalted in the earth" (Ps 46:10).

God who shines on us and in us, provide us with wider vision and greater hope, that we may be freed to trust your presence in all, and for all, through Jesus Christ our Lord.

Amen.

STATION FOURTEEN: A HYMN OF PRAISE

The light shines in the darkness.

And the darkness did not overtake it.

"O sing to the Lord a new song, for he has done marvelous things. His right hand and his holy arm have gotten him victory. The Lord has made known his victory; he has revealed his vindication in the sight of the nations. He has remembered his steadfast love and faithfulness to the house of Israel. All the ends of the earth have seen the victory of our God. Make a joyful noise to the Lord, all the earth; break forth into joyous song and sing praises. Sing praises to the Lord with the lyre, with the lyre and the sound of melody. With trumpets and the sound of the horn make a joyful noise before the King, the Lord. Let the sea roar and all that fills it, the world and those who live in it. Let the floods clap their hands; let the hills sing together for joy at the presence of the Lord, for he is coming to judge the earth. He will judge the world with righteousness and the peoples with equity" (Ps 98:1–9).

[*Silence for personal reflection*]

"Let the peoples praise you, O God;

let all the peoples praise you" (Ps 67:3).

God who shines on us and in us, join our voices to the song of creation, that all we do, and all we are, might proclaim your loving companionships, through Jesus Christ our Lord.

Amen.

CLOSING PRAYERS

"How precious is your steadfast love, O God!

All people may take refuge in the shadow of your wings.

They feast on the abundance of your house,

and you give them drink from the river of your delights.

For with you is the fountain of life;

in your light we see light" (Ps 36:7–9).

The Lord bless us and direct our days and our deeds in peace.

Amen.

Arise, shine; for your light has come,

And the glory of the Lord has risen upon you.

Appendix 2

Stations of the Spirit

A Prayer Journey of Spiritual Gifts or Charisms
Written in 2024 by Laura Marie Piotrowicz

IN ALL STATIONS PRAYERS, we journey through a series of experiences, aspiring to connect with God and each other more deeply in ways that will move us to live out our faith as authentically and enthusiastically as we are able.

This stations prayer is offered as part of discernment of gifts, an act that God invites us into throughout our lives. We recognize that many gifts have been promised by God and are administered by the Holy Spirit. No one will have all gifts, nor are all gifts permanent or perpetual; yet, everyone in the household of God at certain times receives the gift and responsibility of certain charisms. These gifts serve as resources or tools to use in building up the church and increase the spiritual strength and offering of the community. These gifts are not meant to make the people of God competitive,but to offer them increasing ways to be collaborative in the mutual ministry of sharing God's good news.

The gifts in this journey are those identified by St. Paul in his First Letter to the Corinthians, chapter 12. It may be beneficial to read this chapter prior to beginning these stations.

INVOCATION

In the name of God who created us, Christ who redeems us, and Spirit who inspires us,

Amen.

We enter this journey, walking alongside the presence of divine love, seeking quiet minds and open hearts.

"*Lord, to whom can we go? You have the words of eternal life.*

We have come to believe and know that you are the Holy One of God" (John 6:68b–69).

THE LORD'S PRAYER

(Consider alternative versions of the prayer, which may inspire new perspectives on this journey of open-heartedness and seeking, perhaps a paraphrase or one that has been written/compiled from a member of the community.)

"Now there are varieties of gifts, but the same Spirit; and there are varieties of services, but the same Lord; and there are varieties of activities, but it is the same God who activates all of them in everyone. To each is given the manifestation of the Spirit for the common good" (1 Cor 12:4–7).

STATION ONE: RECEIVING WORDS OF WISDOM

"I pray that the God of our Lord Jesus Christ, the Father of glory, may give you a spirit of wisdom and revelation as you come to know him, so that, with the eyes of your heart enlightened, you may know what is the hope to which he has called you, what are the riches of his glorious inheritance among the saints, and what is the immeasurable greatness of his power for us who believe, according to the working of his great power" (Eph 1:17–19).

[*Silence for personal reflection*]

"The wisdom from above is first pure, then peaceable, gentle, willing to yield, full of mercy and good fruits, without a trace of partiality or hypocrisy" (Jas 3:17).

"*It is the Spirit that gives life; . . . the words [of God] are spirit and life*" (from John 6:63).

Let us pray:

Gracious God, you reveal knowledge of your great mysteries, which are too big for us to comprehend. Encourage those who are gifted with this wisdom, that they find new ways to share it, and with others, celebrate your kin-dom as a place of rejoicing in your truth.

God, give us your grace.

STATION TWO: RECEIVING WORDS OF KNOWLEDGE

"Then the mystery was revealed to Daniel in a vision of the night, and Daniel blessed the God of heaven. Daniel said: 'Blessed be the name of God from age to age, for wisdom and power are his. He changes times and seasons, deposes kings and sets up kings; he gives wisdom to the wise and knowledge to those who have understanding. He reveals deep and hidden things; he knows what is in the darkness, and light dwells with him'" (Dan 2:19–22).

[*Silence for personal reflection*]

"Teach me good judgment and knowledge, for I believe in your commandments" (Ps 119:66).

"It is the Spirit that gives life; . . . the words [of God] are spirit and life."

Let us pray:

Omnipotent God, you know all things and reveal them to your children to be used for the good of all. Teach us your word, that we may understand your truth and apply this knowledge to all we do, in your name.

God, give us your grace.

STATION THREE: POSSESSING EXCEPTIONAL FAITH

"'My righteous one will live by faith. My soul takes no pleasure in anyone who shrinks back.' But we are not among those who shrink back and so are lost, but among those who have faith and so are saved. Now faith is the assurance of things hoped for, the conviction of things not seen. Indeed, by faith our ancestors received approval. By faith we understand that the worlds were prepared by the word of God, so that what is seen was made from things that are not visible" (Heb 10:38–11:3).

[*Silence for personal reflection*]

"By grace you have been saved through faith, and this is not your own doing; it is the gift of God" (Eph 2:8).

"It is the Spirit that gives life; . . . the words [of God] are spirit and life."

Let us pray:

Faithful God, you bless all who put their trust in you. For those empowered with extraordinary faith, may they use this exceptional gift to inspire others to live in the assurance and comfort of your truth and power.

God, give us your grace.

STATION FOUR: GIFTS OF HEALING

"When Jesus had come down from the mountain, great crowds followed him; and there was a leper who came to him and knelt before him, saying, 'Lord, if you choose, you can make me clean.' He stretched out his hand and touched him, saying, 'I do choose. Be made clean!' Immediately his leprosy was cleansed. . . . When he entered Capernaum, a centurion came to him, appealing to him and saying, 'Lord, my servant is lying at home paralysed, in terrible distress.' And he said to him, 'I will come and cure him.' . . . And to the centurion Jesus said, 'Go; let it be done for you according to your faith.' And the servant was healed in that hour. When Jesus entered Peter's house, he saw his mother-in-law lying in bed with a fever; he touched her hand, and the fever left her, and she got up and began to serve him. That evening they brought to him many who were possessed by demons; and he cast out the spirits with a word, and cured all who were sick. This was to fulfil what had been spoken through the prophet Isaiah, 'He took our infirmities and bore our diseases'" (Matt 8:1–3, 5–7, 13–17).

[*Silence for personal reflection*]

"Heal me, O Lord, and I shall be healed; save me, and I shall be saved; for you are my praise" (Jer 17:14).

"It is the Spirit that gives life; . . . the words [of God] are spirit and life."

Let us pray:

Loving God, though many seek a medical fix, you offer us spiritual wholeness and peace. Through the hands of those with this gift of healing, may your power and presence be known; may your mercy and love be felt; may the assurance of your promises be a balm to the soul.

God, give us your grace.

STATION FIVE: MIRACLES

"Believe me that I am in the Father and the Father is in me; but if you do not, then believe me because of the works themselves. Very truly, I tell you, the one who believes in me will also do the works that I do and, in fact, will do greater works than these, because I am going to the Father. I will do whatever you ask in my name, so that the Father may be glorified in the Son. If in my name you ask me for anything, I will do it" (John 14:11–14).

[*Silence for personal reflection*]

"Grant to your servants to speak your word with all boldness, while you stretch out your hand to heal, and signs and wonders are performed through the name of your holy servant Jesus" (Acts 4:29b–30).

"*It is the Spirit that gives life; . . . the words [of God] are spirit and life.*"

Let us pray:

God of wonders, help us to celebrate the everyday miracles in our lives. May we respect that all miracles are individual events in your time and choosing, and help us to be supportive of those people you have chosen to be conduits of your extraordinary involvement.

God, give us your grace.

STATION SIX: PROPHESY

"You shall eat in plenty and be satisfied, and praise the name of the Lord your God, who has dealt wondrously with you. And my people shall never again be put to shame. You shall know that I am in the midst of Israel, and that I, the Lord, am your God and there is no other. And my people shall never again be put to shame. Then afterwards I will pour out my spirit on all flesh; your sons and your daughters shall prophesy, your old men shall dream dreams, and your young men shall see visions. Even on the male and female slaves, in those days, I will pour out my spirit" (Joel 2:26–29).

[*Silence for personal reflection*]

"Then the Lord said to me, 'Prophesy to these bones, and say to them: O dry bones, hear the word of the Lord'" (Ezek 37:4).

"*It is the Spirit that gives life; . . . the words [of God] are spirit and life.*"

Let us pray:

Revealing God, you gift us with prophets who are given voice to speak your divine truth to our human ears. May we truly hear these messages, and by them, be strengthened for service to your whole creation.

God, give us your grace.

STATION SEVEN: DISCERNMENT OF SPIRITS

"Beloved, do not believe every spirit, but test the spirits to see whether they are from God; for many false prophets have gone out into the world. By this you know the Spirit of God: every spirit that confesses that Jesus Christ has come in the flesh is from God. . . . Little children, you are from God, and have conquered them; for the one who is in you is greater than the one who is in the world. They are from the world; therefore what they say is from the world, and the world listens to them. We are from God. Whoever knows God listens to us, and whoever is not from God does not listen to us. From this we know the spirit of truth and the spirit of error" (1 John 4:1–2, 4–6).

[*Silence for personal reflection*]

"Do not quench the Spirit. Do not despise the words of prophets, but test everything; hold fast to what is good; abstain from every form of evil" (1 Thess 5:19–22).

"*It is the Spirit that gives life; . . . the words [of God] are spirit and life.*"

Let us pray:

Guiding God, as we discern how to love fully in our ministries, we ask your blessing on those whose gift is to distinguish the nature of the forces of this world. May their guidance help us to reject hurtful actions and lead us only to those things which build up your kin-dom.

God, give us your grace.

STATION EIGHT: SPEAKING IN TONGUES

"Divided tongues, as of fire, appeared among them, and a tongue rested on each of them. All of them were filled with the Holy Spirit and began to speak in other languages, as the Spirit gave them ability. Now there were devout Jews from every nation under heaven living in Jerusalem. And at this sound the crowd gathered and was bewildered, because each one heard them speaking in the native language of each. Amazed and astonished, they asked, 'Are not all these who are speaking Galileans? And how is it that we hear, each of us, in our own native language? Parthians, Medes, Elamites, and residents of Mesopotamia, Judea and Cappadocia, Pontus and Asia, Phrygia and Pamphylia, Egypt and the parts of Libya belonging to Cyrene, and visitors from Rome, both Jews and proselytes, Cretans and Arabs—in our own languages we hear them speaking about God's deeds of power'" (Acts 2:3–11).

[*Silence for personal reflection*]
"When Paul had laid his hands on them, the Holy Spirit came upon them, and they spoke in tongues" (Acts 19:6).

"It is the Spirit that gives life; . . . the words [of God] are spirit and life."
Let us pray:
God, you speak to us in ways that we understand, and in ways that confound us. May those who are given the gift of tongues use this charism wisely and appropriately, not for personal glorification but for the betterment of our community.

God, give us your grace.

STATION NINE: INTERPRETING OF TONGUES

"What should be done then, my friends? When you come together, each one has a hymn, a lesson, a revelation, a tongue, or an interpretation. Let all things be done for building up. If anyone speaks in a tongue, let there be only two or at most three, and each in turn; and let one interpret. But if there is no one to interpret, let them be silent in church and speak to themselves and to God" (1 Cor 14:26–28).

[*Silence for personal reflection*]
"Therefore, one who speaks in a tongue should pray for the power to interpret" (1 Cor 14:13).

"It is the Spirit that gives life; . . . the words [of God] are spirit and life."
Let us pray:
God of companionship, you provide those with this gift the opportunity and responsibility to interpret your words; may they serve you in authentic and fulfilling ways.

God, give us your grace.

STATION TEN: SERVICE AS AN APOSTLE/EVANGELIST

"Then Jesus called the twelve together and gave them power and authority over all demons and to cure diseases, and he sent them out to proclaim the kingdom of God and to heal. He said to them, 'Take nothing for your journey, no staff, nor bag, nor bread, nor money—not even an extra tunic. Whatever house you enter, stay there, and leave from there. Wherever they do not welcome you, as you are leaving that town shake the dust off your feet as a testimony against them.' They departed and went through the villages, bringing the good news and curing diseases everywhere" (Luke 9:1–6).

[*Silence for personal reflection*]

"[Jesus] said to them, 'Go into all the world and proclaim the good news to the whole creation'" (Mark 16:15).

"*It is the Spirit that gives life; . . . the words [of God] are spirit and life.*"

Let us pray:

Encourager, you gift some with the message to go forth into unique service, motivating faith-filled endurance, building of healthy community, and leading us to good works. As they are sent, may we receive them; and may your will be done as they live your good news.

God, give us your grace.

STATION ELEVEN: TEACHING AND PREACHING

"Give ear, O heavens, and I will speak; let the earth hear the words of my mouth. May my teaching drop like the rain, my speech condense like the dew; like gentle rain on grass, like showers on new growth. For I will proclaim the name of the Lord; ascribe greatness to our God!" (Deut 32:1–3).

[*Silence for personal reflection*]

"Let the word of Christ dwell in you richly; teach and admonish one another in all wisdom; and with gratitude in your hearts sing psalms, hymns, and spiritual songs to God" (Col 3:16).

"*It is the Spirit that gives life; . . . the words [of God] are spirit and life.*"

Let us pray:

Instructing God, your Son offered teaching and preaching without bounds, and you continue to inspire us to follow his example. As those teachers are blessed, so, too, is the church blessed to receive a gifted teacher. We thank you for empowering these in our midst.

God, give us your grace.

STATION TWELVE: ADMINISTRATION

"I exhort the elders among you to tend the flock of God that is in your charge, exercising the oversight, not under compulsion but willingly, as God would have you do it—not for sordid gain but eagerly. Do not lord it over those in your charge, but be examples to the flock. And when the chief shepherd appears, you will win the crown of glory that never fades away" (1 Pet 5:1b–4).

[*Silence for personal reflection*]

"And after they had appointed elders for them in each church, with prayer and fasting they entrusted them to the Lord in whom they had come to believe" (Acts 14:23).

"It is the Spirit that gives life; . . . the words [of God] are spirit and life."

Let us pray:

Holy God, you created order out of chaos. Assist those who seek to govern, that they may do so with compassion and kindness, always striving for peace and justice, and serving for the benefit of all.

God, give us your grace.

STATION THIRTEEN: HELP/SERVICE

"Then the king will say to those at his right hand, 'Come, you that are blessed by my Father, inherit the kingdom prepared for you from the foundation of the world; for I was hungry and you gave me food, I was thirsty and you gave me something to drink, I was a stranger and you welcomed me, I was naked and you gave me clothing, I was sick and you took care of me, I was in prison and you visited me.' . . . And the king will answer them, 'Truly I tell you, just as you did it to one of the least of these who are members of my family, you did it to me'" (Matt 25:34–36, 40).

[*Silence for personal reflection*]

"Only fear the Lord, and serve him faithfully with all your heart; for consider what great things he has done for you" (1 Sam 12:24).

"It is the Spirit that gives life; . . . the words [of God] are spirit and life."

Let us pray:

God, you provide for us those who will help in our need, and those who we can help from our abundance. Bless those who are called to serve others as an extension of the church's collective worship, as both body and soul are nourished.

God, give us your grace.

STATION FOURTEEN: LEADERSHIP

"He established a decree in Jacob, and appointed a law in Israel, which he commanded our ancestors to teach to their children; that the next generation might know them, the children yet unborn, and rise up and tell them to their children, so that they should set their hope in God, and not forget the works of God, but keep his commandments; and that they should not be like their ancestors, a stubborn and rebellious generation, a generation whose heart was not steadfast, whose spirit was not faithful to God" (Ps 78:5–8).

[*Silence for personal reflection*]

"Let the words of my mouth and the meditation of my heart be acceptable to you, O Lord, my rock and my redeemer" (Ps 19:14).

"It is the Spirit that gives life; . . . the words [of God] are spirit and life."

Let us pray:

Ruler of all, you call and foster some to lead your church with diligence and dedication. Strengthen those who initiate and motivate your church, that we may praise you in holiness and righteousness all our days.

God, give us your grace.

CLOSING PRAYER

God, as we leave this place but never leave your presence, may we cherish this time we have spent here.

May we celebrate the spiritual gifts that we have known and shared: the gifts that we see and encourage in others around us, and the gifts that have not yet been revealed deep within us.

May we never take for granted the gifts of the Spirit in our lives.

We come as we are, we share what we have, we celebrate being together in the new life of Christ.

"For as in one body we have many members, and not all the members have the same function, so we, who are many, are one body in Christ, and individually we are members one of another. We have gifts that differ according to the grace given to us" (Rom 12:4–6a).

Divine Love, inspire us to use these gifts.

BLESSING

May God, who loved us all into being, inspire us to love others.

May Jesus, whose work of salvation and redemption never ends, be known as a constant companion on our journey.

May Spirit, who showers these gifts and graces upon us, encourage and uphold us in all we do.

Amen.

Bibliography

Anglican Church of Canada. *Book of Common Prayer*. Toronto: Anglican Book Centre, 1962.

Anglican Council of Indigenous Peoples. *A Disciple's Prayer Book*. Minneapolis: Indigenous Theological Training Institute, 1992. https://www.anglican.ca/wp-content/uploads/a-disciples-prayer-book.pdf.

Catechism of the Catholic Church. Chicago: University of Loyola Press, 1994.

Eckhart, Meister. *The Complete Mystical Works of Meister Eckhart*. Translated by Maurice O'Connell Walshe. New York: Crossroad, 2009.

Evangelical Lutheran Church of America. *Evangelical Lutheran Worship*. Minneapolis: Augsburg Fortress, 2006.

Hervieu-Léger, Danièle. *Religion as a Chain of Memory*. Translated by Simon Lee. New Brunswick, NJ: Rutgers University Press, 2000.

Hurston, Zora Neale. *Dust Tracks on a Road: An Autobiography*. Philadelphia: J. B. Lippincott, 1942.

Johnson, Donald, and Susan Johnson. *Praying the Catechism*. Minneapolis: Augsburg Fortress, 2021.

Lewis, C. S. *The World's Last Night and Other Essays*. New York: Harcourt Brace, 1960.

Luther, Martin. "The Smalcald Articles." In *The Book of Concord: The Confessions of the Evangelical Lutheran Church*, edited by Robert Kolb and Timothy Wengert, 297–328. Minneapolis: Fortress, 2000.

Magnetic Poetry. "Our Story." https://magneticpoetry.com/pages/about-us.

Nouwen, Henri. *Behold the Beauty of the Lord: Praying With Icons*. Notre Dame, IN: Ave Maria, 2007.

Tickle, Phyllis. *The Divine Hours: Prayers for Autumn and Wintertime*. New York: Doubleday, 2000.

———. *The Divine Hours: Prayers for Springtime*. New York: Doubleday, 2001.

———. *The Divine Hours: Prayers for Summertime*. New York: Doubleday, 2000.

Thoreau, Henry David. "Journal 2: Chapter 7." In *The Writings of Henry David Thoreau*, Walden ed., 367–439. Boston: Houghton Mifflin, 1906. https://www.walden.org/wp-content/uploads/2016/02/Journal-2-Chapter-7.pdf.

Thornton, Martin. *Christian Proficiency*. London: SPCK, 1961.

———. *English Spirituality: An Outline of Ascetical Theology According to the English Pastoral Tradition*. London: SPCK, 1963.

———. *The Function of Theology*. London: SPCK, 1968.

———. *Pastoral Theology: A Reorientation*. Eugene, OR: Wipf & Stock, 2010.

Varshney, Pranidhi. "My Take on Cultural Appropriation and Yoga." Yoga Journal, Aug. 12, 2022. https://www.yogajournal.com/yoga-101/cultural-appropriation-yoga/.

Woods, Mark. "Yoga: Spiritually Dangerous or Just a Good Work Out." Christian Today, Feb. 11, 2015. https://www.christiantoday.com/article/yoga.spiritually.dangerous.or.just.a.good.workout/47924.htm.

www.ingramcontent.com/pod-product-compliance
Lightning Source LLC
LaVergne TN
LVHW050649100826
845148LV00011B/2048
9798385272280